ERASE the WASTE and Turn Trash Into Cash

GRADES 3–4

ERASE the WASTE and Turn Trash Into Cash

Inquiry-Based Science Lessons for Advanced and Gifted Students in Grades 3–4

Jason S. McIntosh, Ph.D.

PRUFROCK PRESS INC.
WACO, TEXAS

Edited by Katy McDowall
Editorial Assistant: Andilynn Feddeler

Cover and layout design by Allegra Denbo

ISBN-13: 978-1-64632-097-4

Printed in the United States of America.

Prufrock Press Inc.
P.O. Box 8813
Waco, TX 76714-8813
Phone: (800) 998-2208
Fax: (800) 240-0333
https://www.prufrock.com

Table of Contents

Introduction

Americans throw away 254 million tons of trash every year, and students are naturally curious about where it all goes. *Erase the Waste and Turn Trash Into Cash* is a 30-lesson interdisciplinary science unit designed to teach high-ability third and fourth graders how to think like real-world environmental engineers as they encounter tasks that require them to reduce, reuse, recycle, and reimagine trash in new and innovative ways. The concept of change over time is developed and reinforced in every lesson as students participate in a fictitious reality show called *Waste Warriors*. Activities like "Differentiate the Detritus" guide students through the process of sorting and classifying waste into categories, while others such as "Recycle Fest" and "The Greenness Gauge" empower students to use their creativity and embrace the green economy. Students study the concept of change over time and learn to manage and dispose of waste in creative and environmentally friendly ways. Suggestions and guidance are included on how teachers can adjust the rigor of learning tasks based on students' interests and needs. As the old saying goes, "Give a Hoot! Don't Pollute!" But do not forget: You could also make some LOOT along the way!

Detailed Description of the Unit

Rationale

Erase the Waste and Turn Trash Into Cash was designed around the concept of change over time. Elementary-age students (in particular, third and fourth graders) are developmentally ready to identify complex patterns and critically analyze the impact of human actions on the environment around them. In addition, their conception of time has matured to a level in which productive discussions and valid conclusions can be made from comparing and contrasting past, present, and future events.

How to Differentiate Using This Unit

Erase the Waste and Turn Trash Into Cash provides opportunities for both enriched learning and accelerated instruction. The unit begins with a pretest designed to determine students' prior knowledge of and interest in environmental issues and the concept of change over time. Suggestions for adjusting the learning activities and optional anchor activities for students in need of more challenge are included with almost every lesson. In addition, daily reflection activities have been added to help identify misconceptions students might have and aid in planning for the next lesson. Lastly, the use of flexible grouping for instruction, as well as strategic construction of the problem-based learning workgroups throughout, are recommended.

Goals and Outcomes

Concept Goal: To develop the enduring understandings related to change over time to such a degree that students will have the ability to successfully answer the essential questions that follow.

1. *Enduring understandings*: Change over time:
    - is not always easy,
    - is unavoidable,
    - can be positive or negative,
    - can be slow or fast,
    - can happen naturally or be caused by humans,
    - can be chaotic or orderly, and
    - can be temporary or permanent.

2. *Essential questions*:
    - How do you personally deal with change?
    - What can be done to slow down or accelerate change?
    - What are the causes and effects of a change in your community?
    - Do the benefits of change outweigh the costs?

Students will be able to:
- realistically extrapolate future data from past and present data, and
- understand the degree to which current decisions and behaviors affect the future.

STEM Goal: To develop an understanding of the impact human consumption of resources has on the planet and develop the skills and attitudes of an environmental engineer.

- *Science outcomes*: Students will be able to:
    - explain the importance of conservation due to limited resources,
    - identify the phases in the life cycle of a product (i.e., extraction, production, distribution, consumption, disposal),
    - apply the 4R's to create positive change in a community, and
    - classify waste as either organic, inorganic, recyclable, compostable, reusable, or disposable.

- *Technology outcomes*: Students will be able to:
    - compare and contrast new cutting-edge technologies with outdated processes in the science of waste management, and
    - conduct advanced research using online resources and tools.

- *Engineering outcomes*: Students will be able to:
    - design a plan for reducing unnecessary waste in a complicated system, and
    - apply the SCAMPER technique to build and test a prototype made out of recyclable waste.

- *Math outcomes*: Students will be able to:
    - analyze and complete a general ledger used in business to calculate expenditures and profits, and
    - accurately read and create pie charts, as well as calculate percentages.

Humanities Goal: To understand the importance of personal responsibility and business ethics through reading, writing, listening, and speaking about environmental engineering.

- *Language arts outcomes*: Students will be able to:
  - read and comprehend complex literary and informational texts independently and engage effectively in a range of collaborative discussions (one-on-one, in groups, and teacher-led) with diverse partners building on others' ideas and expressing their own clearly, and
  - produce clear and coherent writing in which the development, organization, and style are appropriate to task, purpose, and audience.

- *Social studies outcomes*: Students will be able to:
  - generate and analyze business plans and marketing campaigns,
  - distinguish between a want and a need in order to identify greed/overconsumption, and
  - recognize and appreciate the value of making connections between businesses, communities, states, and countries.

Process Goal: To develop critical thinking, creative thinking, and social skills. Students will be able to:

- use logical thinking to solve problems and justify solutions,
- develop interpersonal skills while working in groups, and
- develop creativity through art, writing, speaking, and engineering.

Connections to Standards

This unit aligns to the Common Core State Standards (CCSS) for English Language Arts and Mathematics, as well as the Next Generation Science Standards (NGSS). To see specific standards addressed, the end of the unit includes a CCSS alignment chart and an NGSS alignment chart.

This unit also includes connections to the National Association for Gifted Children's 2019 Pre-K–Grade 12 Gifted Programming Standards, including the following:

- **1.3. Self-Understanding.** Students with gifts and talents demonstrate understanding of and respect for similarities and differences between themselves and their cognitive and chronological peer groups and others in the general population.
- **1.5. Cognitive, Psychosocial, and Affective Growth.** Students with gifts and talents demonstrate cognitive growth and psychosocial skills that support their talent development as a result of meaningful and challenging learning activities that address their unique characteristics and needs.

- **2.4. Learning Progress.** As a result of using multiple and ongoing assessments, students with gifts and talents demonstrate growth commensurate with abilities in cognitive, social-emotional, and psychosocial areas.
- **2.5. Learning Progress.** Students self-assess their learning progress.
- **3.5. Instructional Strategies.** Students with gifts and talents become independent investigators.
- **3.6.2. Resources.** Educators use school and community resources to support differentiation and advanced instruction appropriate to students' interests, strengths, and academic learning needs.
- **4.1. Personal Competence.** Students with gifts and talents demonstrate growth in personal competence and dispositions for exceptional academic and creative productivity. These include self-awareness, self-advocacy, self-efficacy, confidence, motivation, resilience, independence, curiosity, and risk taking.
- **4.2. Social Competence.** Students with gifts and talents develop social competence manifested in positive peer relationships and social interactions.
- **4.3. Responsibility and Leadership.** Students with gifts and talents demonstrate personal and social responsibility.
- **5.6.2. Policies and Procedures.** Educators align programming and services with local, state, or national laws, rules, regulations, and standards.

Introduction

LESSON 1

Appraising Prior Knowledge

Objectives

- Students will complete a preassessment.
- Students will be introduced to the concept of change over time.

Materials

- Handout 1.1: Pretest
- Clean trash (10–20 items)
- Butcher paper
- Markers
- Tape
- Student journals (blank notebook for each student)

Assessments

- Preassessment
- Journal prompt

Procedures

1. Greet students as they arrive.
2. Use the following anticipatory set to focus attention and engage learners:
    - Introduce the title of the unit: *Erase the Waste and Turn Trash Into Cash.*
    - Show students a small bag of clean, safe garbage (e.g., empty water bottle, tissue box, orange peel, mayo jar, crumpled newspaper, etc.). Dump the bag of garbage out on a table for students to see.
    - Pose the following question: *How is it possible to turn this trash into real money?*
    - Give students several minutes to talk to a partner about their ideas.
    - Ask for a few volunteers to share their thoughts. Do not confirm or deny the accuracy of any ideas that are shared. Simply listen.
3. Inform students that they will now take a short preassessment designed to determine what they already know about reducing, reusing, recycling, and reimagining waste. Explain that the assessment is not for a grade.
4. Distribute Handout 1.1: Pretest. Give students time to take the pretest. (Collect and score before the next lesson and put away for safekeeping until the last day of class.)
5. As students are taking the preassessment, lay a large piece of butcher paper on the ground in the front of the classroom along with markers, crayons, and colored pencils.
6. Invite students to sit around the butcher paper and collaboratively draw a mural of the most beautiful city park or outdoor green space they can possibly imagine. As soon as the mural is finished, ask students to help you attach the butcher paper mural to the wall using tape.
7. Direct students to return to their seats and then begin to tape the clean garbage you used in the anticipatory set right on top of their mural.
8. Ask students to describe how this makes them feel.

9. Provide students with the following data:
   - According to the Environmental Protection Agency (U.S. EPA, 2016), each American produces 4.4 pounds of trash a day. Only 1.51 pounds of that trash is recycled.
   - According to TheWorldCounts (n.d.), people around the world produce 2.12 billion tons of trash every year.
   - According to National Geographic (Leahy, 2018), people around the world produce 3.5 million tons of plastic and solid waste every day. This is 10 times more than the amount of waste produced a century ago.

10. Challenge students to hypothesize why we produce so many more pounds of trash today as compared to years ago.
11. Write the term *change over time*. Create a class definition and generate a list of three or four generalizations about the idea of change (e.g., change is not always easy, change can be good or bad, change is unavoidable, etc.).
12. Ask students to record the definition and any thoughts they have about what they discussed in this lesson in a notebook or journal.

TEACHER'S NOTE

Hilda Taba created the concept development strategy described in this lesson. For more information on how to use this strategy effectively in your classroom, please read *Concept Development Questioning Strategy: The Taba Approach* by Shelagh A. Gallagher.

Name: ______________________ Date: ______________

HANDOUT 1.1

Pretest

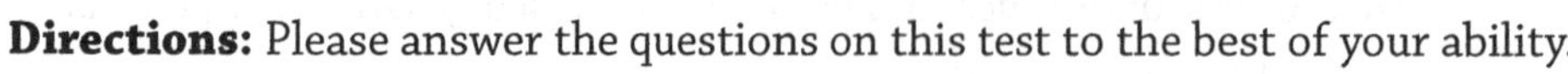

Directions: Please answer the questions on this test to the best of your ability.

1. Give an example of something changing over time.

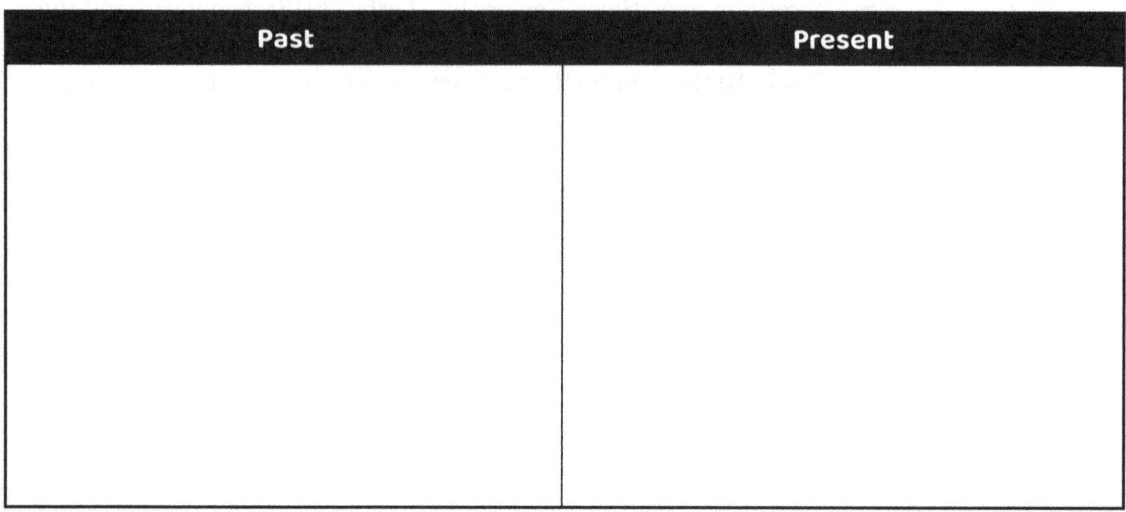

Past	Present

2. What is an *environmental engineer*?

3. List the four tools we can use to erase waste.

4. What does it mean to reimagine something?

LESSON 1

Name: ______________________________ Date: ______________

HANDOUT 1.1, continued

5. What is SCAMPER, and how would you apply it to an empty water bottle?

6. How many pounds of garbage does the average person in the United States create each day?
   a. 1 pound
   b. 2–3 pounds
   c. 4–5 pounds
   d. 6–8 pounds

7. What are two ways you can reduce the amount of trash you produce each day?

8. Define the following terms in your own words:

   a. Throwaway society:

   b. Solid waste management:

   c. Overconsumption:

   d. Compostable:

   e. General ledger:

Name: ______________________________ Date: ______________

HANDOUT 1.1, continued

9. Complete the pie chart below so that it represents an estimate of how much of the garbage produced in the United States is of each type:

   - Metal
   - Plastic
   - Glass
   - Yard trimmings
   - Paper
   - Rubber, leather, fabric
   - Food scraps
   - Wood
   - Other

10. Give three reasons why plastic is such a problem around the world.

11. What are the steps involved in recycling a recyclable item of your choosing (e.g., tin can, plastic water bottle, etc.)?

12. What do you hope to learn during this unit?

LESSON 2

What Is Waste Warriors?

Objectives

- Students will predict the amount of waste created in the United States by type and compare and contrast their predictions with actual EPA data.
- Students will be introduced to the problem-based learning scenario and the goal of thinking like an environmental engineer.

Materials

- Handout 2.1: Pie Chart Predictions
- Handout 2.2: *Waste Warriors* Logo
- Handout 2.3: Need to Know Board
- Student book, computer, and Internet access for research
- Student journals

Assessments

- Journal prompt
- Handout 2.3: Need to Know Board

Procedures

1. Review major concepts from the previous lesson (e.g., definition of change over time, amount of waste produced each year, etc.).
2. Give students several minutes to brainstorm as many types or categories of waste as they can think of with a partner (e.g., paper, plastic, glass, metal, food scraps, lawn clippings, etc.).
3. Ask pairs to share what is on their list without repeating another group.
4. Distribute Handout 2.1: Pie Chart Predictions. Direct each pair of students to complete the first pie chart predicting what percentage of all waste found in American landfills is made up of each type listed.

TEACHER'S NOTE

If students are unfamiliar with how pie charts work, refer to the following website or any other credible source you prefer: https://www.mathsisfun.com/data/pie-charts.html.

5. Provide the most recent data from the EPA so that students can now fill in the second pie chart with the correct percentages (U.S. EPA, n.d.-a):
   - Food is the largest category of waste in landfills at 24%.
   - Plastic is the second largest category at 19%.
   - Paper and paperboard makes up 12%.
   - Yard trimmings make up 7%.
   - Metal makes up 10%.
   - Wood makes up 8%.
   - Textiles (cloth) make up 8%.
   - Glass makes up 5%.
   - "Other" makes up the rest.

6. Ask students to talk about what surprises them the most about the data.
7. Next, ask students to talk with a partner and record in their journals a list of the three types of waste they feel we can most easily reduce in our daily lives. Provide time for groups to share their list and provide a rationale for their choices.
8. Instead of providing the correct answer regarding the types of waste that can be reduced, explain to students that they will work in small groups over the next few days to investigate a problem-based learning scenario designed to help them answer this very question.
9. Explain to students that throughout the unit they will learn to think like *environmental engineers*. Give students a few minutes to research this term and determine what an environmental engineer does.
10. After students have had a chance to share, define environmental engineer as a career in which people develop solutions to problems that protect and improve the health of living organisms and improve the quality of the environment.
11. Ask students to list the skills and abilities they believe environmental engineers need to do their job (e.g., persistence, ability to analyze details, creativity, etc.).
12. Poll students to determine who is ready to begin their training now.
13. Pose the problem-based learning (PBL) scenario below by reading the following script to the class:

> How many of you love reality shows on television? There are so many to choose from nowadays, such as *American Idol*, *Flip or Flop*, *Dancing With the Stars*, *Property Brothers*, *Project Runway*, *Survivor*, *Be Our Chef*, and so many more. Now, imagine you receive a phone call from the producers of a new hit reality show called *Waste Warriors*. The person on the phone tells you, "We have been searching for a new cast member to join the show on a trial basis. You have been recommended to us because of your excellent work as an environmental engineer. (Display Handout 2.2: *Waste Warriors* Logo for the pretend reality competition.) The premise of the show is unlike any other that has ever been on TV. In each episode, three small businesses from one small town will compete against each other with guidance from cast members of the show to reduce the most waste. The winning team will win $25,000 and the chance to return during the season finale to compete for one million dollars!

14. Divide students into three teams.

TEACHER'S NOTE

Teams can be constructed in multiple ways. Consider using one of the following methods based on the needs of your students:

- create teams based on personalities of students and strengths/weaknesses,
- have students create their own teams,
- use a randomizer to create completely random teams of students, or
- give a student-friendly personality assessment and group students by the results.

15. Distribute Handout 2.3: Need to Know Board. Ask students to record in Column 1 everything they know about the competition and their involvement.
16. Next, ask students to record in Column 2 what they will need to know in order to decide if they will accept the cast position and successfully compete in the challenge.
17. **Journal prompt:** Ask students to complete the following journal prompt: *What would be the best thing about becoming a famous television star? What would be the worst?*

Name: ______________________________ Date: ______________

HANDOUT 2.1

Pie Chart Predictions

Part A

Directions: A pie chart is a graph used to show the percentage of a whole something represents. The more of something there is, the larger the slice of the circle it is given. Think about all of the garbage produced in the United States every year. Create different sized slices in the circle shown below to represent which types of trash we create more of as compared to others. Make sure to label or color code each slice.

Amount of Waste by Type (Prediction)

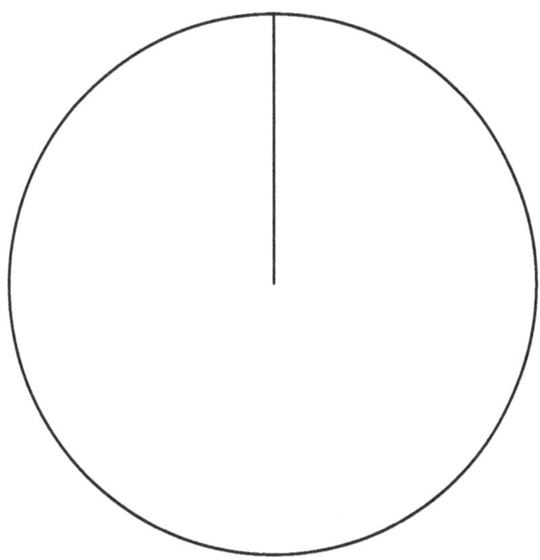

Key

Type	Color
Paper	
Metal	
Glass	
Food	
Plastic	

Type	Color
Textiles	
Yard Trimmings	
Wood	
Other	

Name: ______________________ Date: ______________

Part B

Directions: Your teacher will give you the actual percentage for each type of waste. Record the data in the chart. Next, use the colors in the key on the previous page to create slices that would be close to the size of the percentage of the whole each type actually represents.

Amount of Waste by Type (Actual)

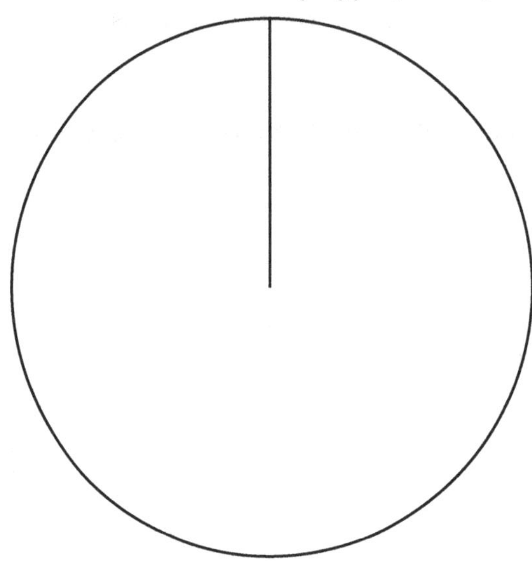

Actual Data by Type

Type	%
Paper	
Metal	
Glass	
Food	
Plastic	

Type	%
Textiles	
Yard Trimmings	
Wood	
Other	

HANDOUT 2.2

Waste Warriors Logo

Tuesdays @ 8:00 p.m.

LESSON 2

Name: ______________________________ Date: ______________

HANDOUT 2.3

Need to Know Board

Directions: List what you know in the first column. Then list what you need to know in the second column and how you can find out in the third. Check off the fourth column when you have learned what you need to know.

What We Know	What We Need to Know	Where We Can Find Out	✓
		Assigned to: ______________	
		Assigned to: ______________	
		Assigned to: ______________	
		Assigned to: ______________	
		Assigned to: ______________	
		Assigned to: ______________	
		Assigned to: ______________	

LESSON 3

Business Plan Bonanza

Objectives

- Students will preview the business plans for three businesses.
- Students will generate a problem statement for the PBL scenario.

Materials

- Handout 2.2: *Waste Warriors* Logo
- Handout 2.3: Need to Know Board
- Handout 3.1: Rosalyn's Restaurant Business Plan
- Handout 3.2: Charlie's Toy Chest Business Plan
- Handout 3.3: M&B Motel Business Plan
- Student journals

Assessments

- Journal prompt
- Problem statements
- Handout 2.3: Need to Know Board

Procedures

1. Review major concepts from the previous lesson (e.g., amount of each type of waste produced each year, what is an environmental engineer, etc.).
2. Ask students to list the questions they recorded in the "What We Need to Know" column of Handout 2.3: Need to Know Board. Provide answers to each question in order to help students decide if they will join the cast of the *Waste Warriors* reality show or not.

TEACHER'S NOTE

Simply make up your own answers to questions pertaining to salary, benefits, hours, etc. If you need time to conduct some research, write the question down and tell students you will get in touch with the producers and get back with them tomorrow.

3. Once each group of students has agreed to join the cast, continue with the next portion of the scenario. Read the following script:

> Congratulations on joining the team! The producers of the show and the two existing cast members cannot wait to work with you. Your first day on the set is next week. In preparation for the upcoming episode, you are given a preview of the three businesses that will be featured. Take a look at the business plan for each one: M&B Motel,

Charlie's Toy Chest, and Rosalyn's Restaurant. Determine as a team which of the three you would like to work with and record what you know and need to know in order to provide assistance to them on Handout 2.3: Need to Know Board.

4. Distribute the business plan handouts (Handouts 3.1–3.3, one of each to all teams), and explain why business plans are written. In short, all businesses provide a solution to a problem or fulfill a need. The business plan describes what solutions each company provides and how they plan to implement them.
5. Remind students that they will be taking on the role of an environmental engineer. Their job is to analyze the business plans and propose solutions to reduce waste. Make sure to give ample time for groups to discuss and record information from the business plans onto their copies of Handout 2.3: Need to Know Board.
6. Debrief with each group and attempt to ensure all three businesses have been assigned to at least one group of students.
7. Ask students to imagine their boss has texted them and asked for a one-sentence summary of their current task. Direct students to get out their journals and work together to craft that sentence together. An example might be: *Advise a business on ways to reduce waste but increase profit.*
8. Provide time for each group to share their sentence. Use this as an opportunity to make sure every student understands the task.
9. **Journal prompt:** Ask students to complete the following journal prompt: *What is one obvious suggestion you, as an environmental engineer, could offer your business owner now?*

TEACHER'S NOTE

It is strongly encouraged that teachers take photographs or videos of students throughout the unit. These photos and videos of projects, presentations, and work sessions can be used to create a highlight reel that will truly enhance the end of the unit/episode celebration incorporated into Lesson 29.

Name: ______________________________ Date: ______________

HANDOUT 3.1

Rosalyn's Restaurant Business Plan

Identity (Who We Are)	**Problem (Needs We Fill)**
At Rosalyn's, we treat you like family! Never pretentious, we provide classic American dishes quickly and economically.	Fast, friendly service in a sit-down restaurant is increasingly uncommon. We provide both!
Our Solution (Services We Provide) Time and cost-cutting measures include: ▪ Buying processed foods in bulk that can be reheated quickly. ▪ Anticipating the number of meals needed each day and preparing them in advance and placing them under heat lamps. ▪ Using disposable utensils, plates, and cups to decrease the time needed to clean. ▪ Requiring "friendliness" training for all staff.	**Target Market (Who We Are Selling to)** The target audience is a family on a budget with a busy schedule that still enjoys sit-down restaurants and classic foods.
The Competition High-priced restaurants and low-priced fast food franchises.	**Revenue Streams (How We Make Money)** ▪ Daily food sales ▪ Customer tips
Marketing Activities A sign out front of the restaurant prominently advertises weekly specials. A commercial is aired on the local radio station. Ads are placed in the Sunday edition of the newspaper.	**Expenses** ▪ Utilities (water, electricity, waste, etc.) ▪ Payroll for staff ▪ Advertising and marketing ▪ Utensils, plates, cups, to-go containers, napkins, packets of condiments, straws ▪ Food from a large American factory three states away ▪ Beverage concentrates and soda ▪ Cleaning products ▪ Rent for the use of a second large outdoor freezer
Team and Key Roles ▪ The owner of the restaurant ▪ Two managers ▪ 12 employees ▪ Bookkeeper ▪ Night guard	**Milestones (Future Long-Term Goals)** Begin offering delivery service or serve breakfast on the weekends.

Name: ______________________ Date: ______________

HANDOUT 3.2

Charlie's Toy Chest Business Plan

Identity (Who We Are)	**Problem (Needs We Fill)**
Charlie's Toy Chest sells inexpensive retro style and modern-day toys for children aged 2–9 years old, 24 hours a day, 7 days a week. We are the only toy store in the nation to offer "sibling insurance" (see Problem section for details).	All kids know what it feels like to have a brother, sister, or friend break or lose their toys. There is nothing worse than finishing a puzzle only to find out three pieces are missing, or going to grab your favorite stuffed animal that is now missing an ear. We offer our customers "sibling insurance," free replacement of any lost/broken toys, for a small one-time 15% upcharge.
Our Solution (How We Reduced Prices)	**Target Market (Who We Are Selling to)**
Instead of purchasing more durable toys, we import cheap products from China and India. We can purchase twice as many for the same amount of money we would spend on quality toys. We also count on a large portion of those who purchase the insurance neglecting to follow through with making a "claim."	The target audience is families with multiple children who value smart spending, longevity of investment, and opportunities to reduce potential conflict.
The Competition	**Revenue Streams (How We Make Money)**
The big box stores like Walmart and Target buy a large volume of toys and therefore can negotiate lower prices.	Charlie's Toy Chest will sell directly to customers inside the physical store.
Marketing Activities	**Expenses**
Charlie's Toy Chest will communicate with customers using social media platforms, email, weekly full-color ads in the local newspaper, a large billboard next to the highway, and paper flyers posted around town.	▪ Contracts with the manufacturers of toys ▪ Shipping costs ▪ Leasing store space ▪ Utilities (waste removal, electricity, etc.) ▪ Payroll for staff ▪ Advertising and marketing
Team and Key Roles	**Milestones (Future Long-Term Goals)**
▪ The owner of the store ▪ Six sales associates to sell the merchandise ▪ An accountant ▪ A janitor	Earn enough profit to purchase the building the store is in.

Name: ______________________ Date: ______________

HANDOUT 3.3

M&B Motel Business Plan

Identity (Who We Are)	Problem (Needs We Fill)
We treat you like a celebrity by providing day and night butler/maid service to fulfill all your traveling needs.	People like to be waited on and pampered when they are away from home.
Our Solution (Services We Provide)	**Target Market (Who We Are Selling to)**
Three full-time maids and butlers are available at all times to provide: ▪ Fresh towels. ▪ Bottles of water, coffee pods, sugar, cream, and Styrofoam cups for the coffee machine. ▪ Unlimited free laundry service. ▪ Extra toiletries (soap, shampoo, etc.). ▪ Food delivered from the five fast food restaurants nearby.	The target audience is a traveler on a budget who is not used to high-quality service.
The Competition	**Revenue Streams (How We Make Money)**
High-priced hotels with excellent service *and* low-priced motels with mediocre to poor service.	Nightly rates for rooms plus tips from guests
Marketing Activities	**Expenses**
Maid and Butler Motel will advertise online, place flyers in the rest stops and truck stops along the highway, and pay to have an airplane fly a banner over stadiums in which football and baseball games are being held.	▪ Utilities (water, electricity, waste, etc.) ▪ Payroll for staff ▪ Advertising and marketing ▪ Toiletries, coffee, water bottles for guests ▪ Gasoline for the butlers to drive to the restaurants for the guests ▪ Groundskeeper, pool cleaner ▪ Taxes to the city
Team and Key Roles	**Milestones (Future Long-Term Goals)**
▪ The owner of the motel ▪ Nine maids and butlers who rotate throughout the week ▪ Maintenance people ▪ Front desk clerk	Expand into other cities.

LESSON 4

The 4R's

Objectives

- Students will brainstorm examples of reducing, reusing, recycling, and reimagining waste.
- Students will apply the 4R's to their own lives.

Materials

- Handout 2.2: *Waste Warriors* Logo
- Handout 2.3: Need to Know Board
- Handout 3.1: Rosalyn's Restaurant Business Plan
- Handout 3.2: Charlie's Toy Chest Business Plan
- Handout 3.3: M&B Motel Business Plan
- Handout 4.1: Poster Set (Reduce, Reuse, Recycle, Reimagine)

- Handout 4.2: 4R's Think Sheet
- Handout 4.3: 4R's Advertising
- Student journals

Assessments

- Handout 2.3: Need to Know Board
- Handout 4.2: 4R's Think Sheet
- Journal prompt

Procedures

1. Review major concepts from the previous lesson (e.g., problem statement, three business plans, etc.).
2. Display the four posters from Handout 4.1: Poster Set (Reduce, Reuse, Recycle, Reimagine).
3. Ask students to work in small groups to create a definition for each word.
4. Give each group an opportunity to share their definitions. Come to a consensus as a whole class as to what the operational definitions will be going forward. Examples include:
   - **Reduce:** Use less of.
   - **Reuse:** Use more than once.
   - **Recycle:** Remake into a new form.
   - **Reimagine:** Rethink and creatively use something.

5. Explain to students that these four tools (i.e., the 4R's—reduce, reuse, recycle, reimagine) are the keys environmental engineers often use to erase waste and turn trash into cash. Provide students an example of how to apply the 4R's using a plastic grocery sack:
   - **Reduce:** Use cloth bags to carry groceries from the store.
   - **Reuse:** Use the plastic bag from the store to take your lunch to school.
   - **Recycle:** Collect and return to a recycling center.
   - **Reimagine:** Create a parachute for an action figure.

6. Display the *Waste Warriors* logo once again (Handout 2.2). With the whole group, list the types of trash the logo features (e.g., plastic, cardboard, metal, food, etc.).

7. Distribute Handout 4.2: 4R's Think Sheet. Challenge students to work independently or in small groups to choose one piece of waste pictured in the logo and apply the 4R's in as many ways as they can.

TEACHER'S NOTE

At this point in the lesson, it might be a good idea to introduce students to the four elements of creativity (i.e., fluency, flexibility, originality, elaboration). Explain to students that the primary purpose of this task is to demonstrate fluency (or many) ideas.

8. A few minutes before ending this activity, ask each group of students to circle their favorite idea in each of the four quadrants. Provide time to share what students circled.
9. Ask students to break into their PBL groups. Using the images on Handout 4.3: 4R's Advertising, give Advertisement A to those working on M&B Motel, Advertisement B to those working on Rosalyn's Restaurant, and Advertisement C to those working on Charlie's Toy Chest. Challenge students to think like environmental engineers and determine which of the 4R's the establishment in their picture is trying to address.
10. Give students the rest of the class period to review the business plans they were given in the previous lesson and generate potential ideas for erasing waste. All ideas should be logged in their journals or on a new copy of the 4R's Think Sheet (Handout 4.2).

TEACHER'S NOTE

Remind students to record specific details they learn about ideas they research on their Need to Know Boards (Handout 2.3).

11. **Journal prompt:** Ask students to complete the following journal prompt: *What are three ways you could reduce, reuse, recycle, or reimagine waste you create on a daily basis? What steps will you take to make this happen?*

Name: ______________________ Date: ______________

HANDOUT 4.1

Poster Set (Reduce, Reuse, Recycle, Reimagine)

REDUCE

REDUCE

REDUCE

REDUCE

Name: ______________________________ Date: ______________

HANDOUT 4.1, continued

LESSON 4

Name: ________________________________ Date: ________________

HANDOUT 4.1, continued

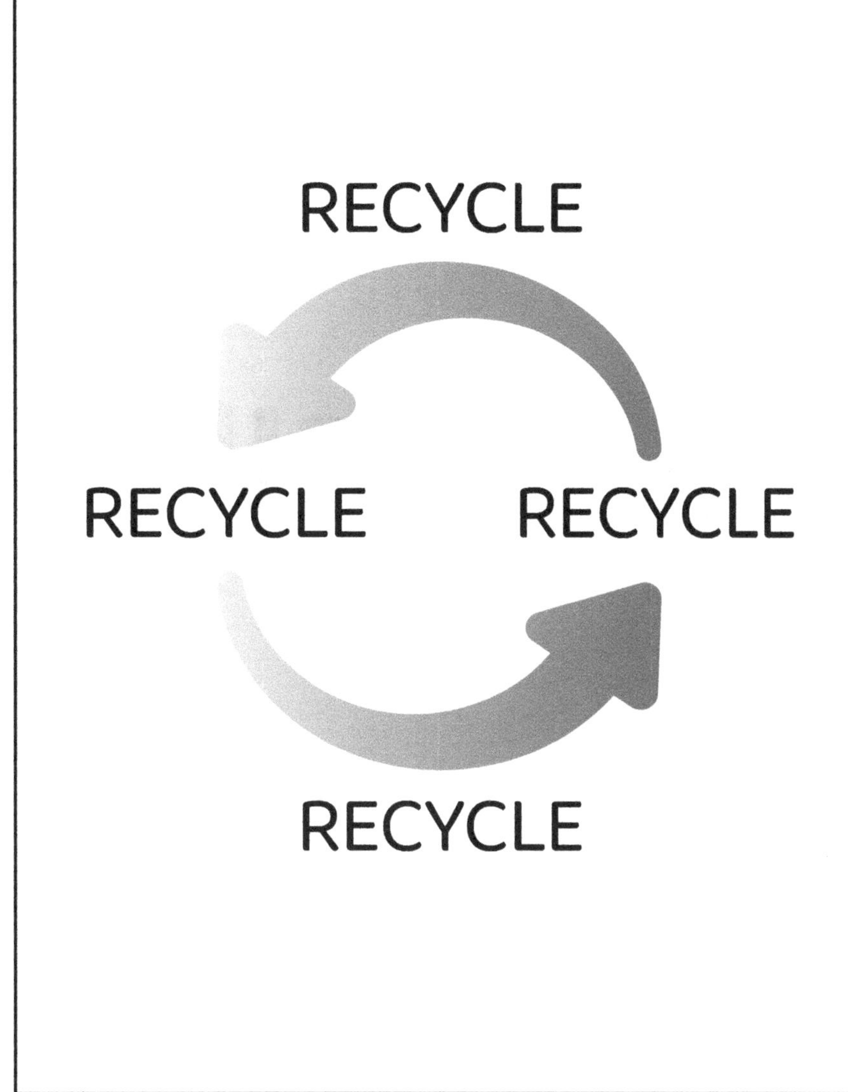

LESSON 4

Name: ______________________________ Date: ______________

HANDOUT 4.1, continued

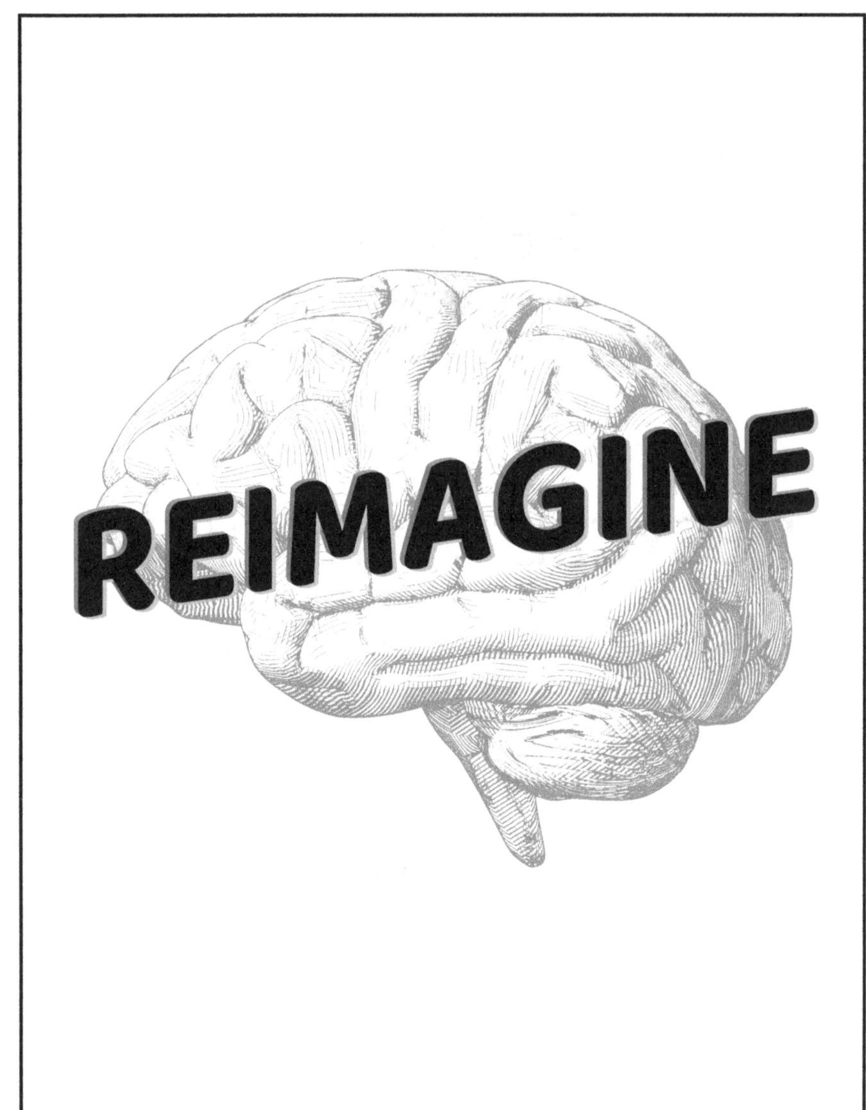

LESSON 4

Name: ______________________________ Date: ______________

HANDOUT 4.2

4R's Think Sheet

Directions: Brainstorm as many ways as you can think of to reduce, reuse, recycle, or reimagine something. Begin by listing what you are pondering in the middle square.

REDUCE
REDUCE
REDUCE
REDUCE

I am pondering ways to reduce, reuse, recycle, and reimagine the following:

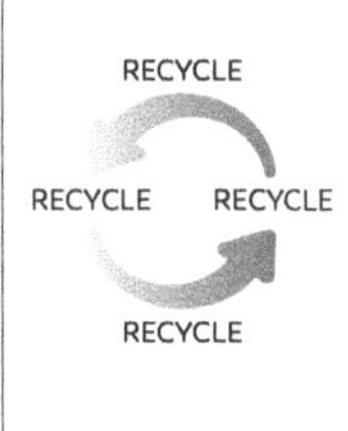

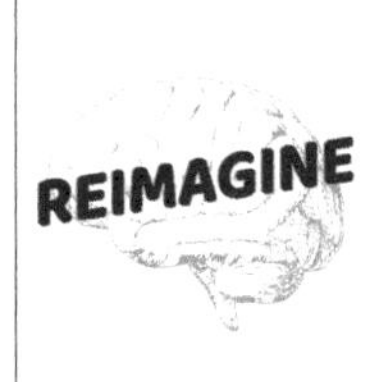

LESSON 4

Name: ______________________________ Date: ______________

HANDOUT 4.3

4R's Advertising

Advertisement A

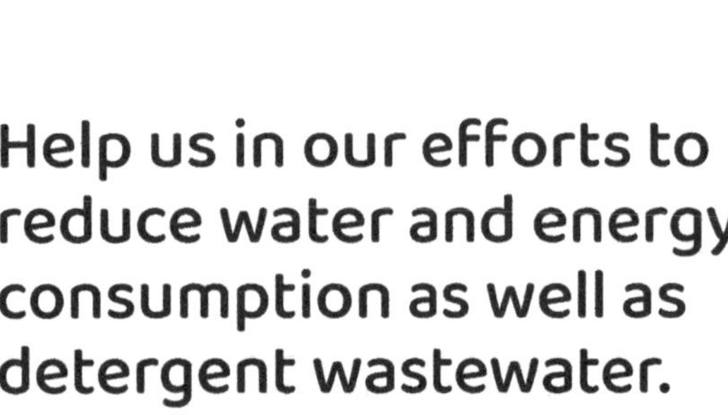

- Towels on the rack mean "I will use again"
- Towels on the floor mean "Please replace"

Each person **CAN** make a difference . . .
Help us make a difference today!

Name: ______________________________ Date: ______________

HANDOUT 4.3, continued

Advertisement B

PIZZA HOUSE is now practicing sustainability by COMPOSTING all food waste at the city's recycling center!

We also broke up with our trash dumpster and are only using a RECYCLING bin. Thanks for joining us on this quest to be a ZERO WASTE restaurant!

Name: ______________________ Date: ______________

Advertisement C

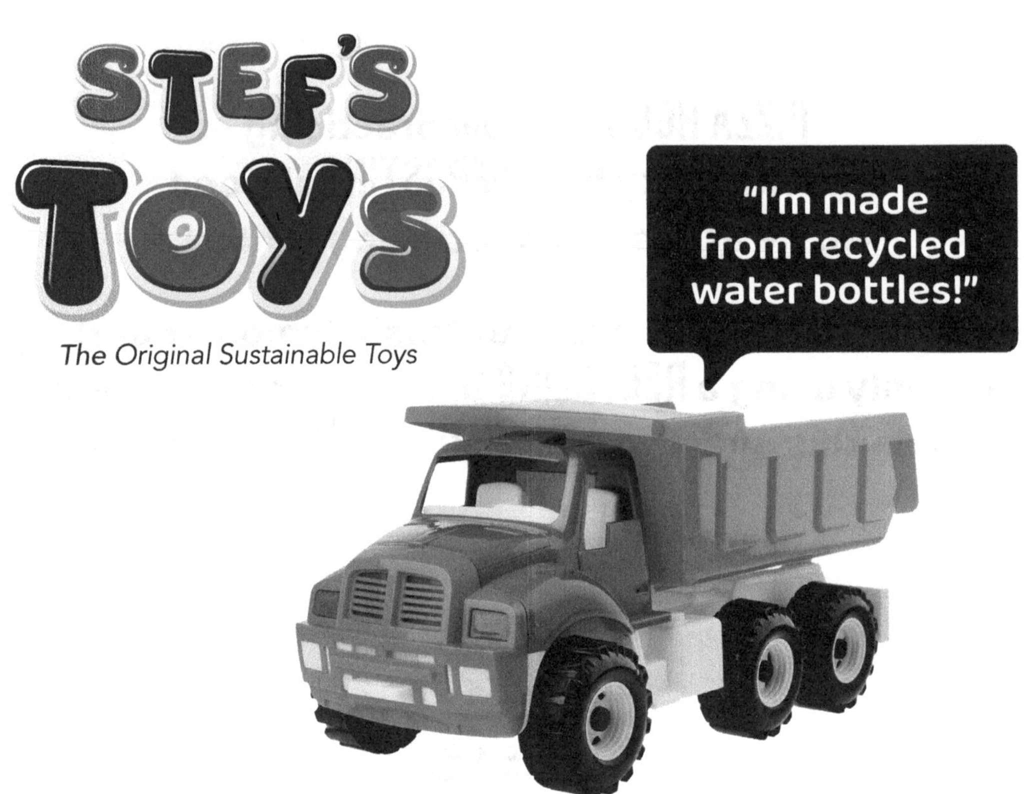

LESSON 5

The Meet and Greet

Objectives

- Students will be introduced to the format of the *Waste Warriors* television show.
- Students will meet the clients they will be advising.

Materials

- Handout 2.3: Need to Know Board
- Handout 5.1: Meet Rosalyn
- Handout 5.2: Meet Charlie
- Handout 5.3: Meet Sylvia and Mark
- Handout 5.4: Current Logos and Slogans
- Student journals

Assessments

- Handout 2.3: Need to Know Board
- Journal prompt

Procedures

1. Review major concepts from the previous lesson (e.g., definitions of reduce, reuse, recycle, reimagine, etc.).
2. Introduce students to the next phase of the PBL scenario by reading the following script:

> Today is a big day! Filming will begin on your first episode. The producers of the show pull you aside and explain the format of each episode. They say that all reality shows have a scripted format that repeats each week. *Waste Warriors* is no exception. Every one-hour episode contains the following six segments:
>
> - **Meet and Greet:** The cast meets the business owners for the first time.
> - **Differentiate the Detritus:** The cast tours the business, examines business plans, observes processes, and analyzes the waste produced.
> - **Look at the Books:** Cast members examine the financials of their business.
> - **Recommendation Roundup:** The cast generates ideas for waste reduction and presents these to the business owners.
> - **Tally Time:** All three teams are scored and ranked.
> - **Bonus Round:** One final challenge determines the winner of the episode.
>
> Today is Day 1. Therefore, you will meet your business owner in one hour. You are excited, but nervous and simply say, "Thanks for the information. Wish me luck!" The producers smile, pat you on the back, and hurriedly walk away, leaving you with your thoughts.

3. Direct students to get into their PBL groups. Distribute Handout 5.1: Meet Rosalyn to the Rosalyn's Restaurant group, Handout 5.2: Meet Charlie to the Charlie's Toy Chest group, and Handout 5.3: Meet Sylvia and Mark to the M&B Motel group.
4. Ask students to read and discuss their handouts and then record what they now know about their business and what they will need to learn on their Need to Know Boards (Handout 2.3).
5. After no fewer than 10 minutes of work time, assign the next task. Groups will generate and write down a list of questions they would like to ask their business owners if they were able to actually interview them in real life. Suggest to students that they pull questions directly from their "What We Need to Know" column on their Need to Know Boards.
6. After several minutes, give groups the opportunity to share a few of the questions they wrote down with the whole class.
7. Collect the list of questions.

TEACHER'S NOTE

Between now and the next lesson, create answers to as many of students' interview questions as you can. A few examples are listed below:

- How much do you pay your maids and butlers each hour? (Minimum wage plus tips.)
- What percentage of customers choose to buy the optional "sibling insurance"? (60%.)
- What types of food do they serve at the chain restaurant next door to Rosalyn's Restaurant? (Soup, salad, burgers, and fries.)

8. Draw students' attention to the advertising and marketing section of their group's business plan. Pose the following questions: *Will these marketing strategies result in new customers that align with the target audience for the business? If not, with what would you replace them?*
9. Provide the following considerations to help students answer the question. Students should consider:

- social media marketing campaigns;
- contest promotions;
- unusual sponsorships;
- coupons or frequent shopper cards;
- print, radio, and TV advertising; and
- celebrity endorsements.

10. Show students Handout 5.4: Current Logos and Slogans for their businesses and challenge them to design a new updated version.

TEACHER'S NOTE

Students may not have time to complete the logo/slogan task during this lesson time. Use this task as an anchor activity going forward. This would entail asking students to come back to this task if they finish other assignments before other students.

11. Debrief the tasks completed today and offer students one more opportunity to record any information on their Need to Know Boards (Handout 2.3).
12. **Journal prompt:** Ask students to complete the following journal prompt: *The United States has laws regarding advertising to children. Why do you think that is?*

Name: ______________________ Date: ______________

HANDOUT 5.1

Meet Rosalyn

Name: ______________________________ Date: ______________

HANDOUT 5.2

Meet Charlie

LESSON 5

Name: ______________________ Date: ______________

HANDOUT 5.3

Meet Sylvia and Mark

LESSON 5

Name: ______________________________ Date: ______________

HANDOUT 5.4

Current Logos and Slogans

Rosalyn's Restaurant

Rosalyn's

RESTAURANT

Charlie's Toy Chest

Charlie's

TOY CHEST

M&B Motel

Where We Treat You Like Royalty

LESSON 5

LESSON 6

Differentiate the Detritus

Objectives

- Students will categorize the waste produced by their business as either organic/inorganic, recyclable, compostable, or reusable.
- Students will analyze the data they collected and determine percentages for each category.

Materials

- Handout 2.3: Need to Know Board
- Handout 6.1: Trash Investigation Inventory
- Handout 6.2: Differentiate the Detritus
- Student book, computer, and Internet access for research
- Student journals

Assessments

- Handout 2.3: Need to Know Board
- Handout 6.2: Differentiate the Detritus
- Journal prompt

Procedures

1. Review major concepts from the previous lesson (e.g., the business owners' personal stories, marketing/advertising techniques, etc.).
2. Share with students the answers to the questions you generated after the previous lesson. Provide time for each group to record the answers on the "know" section of their Need to Know Boards (Handout 2.3).
3. Explain to students that today's segment of the show is called "Differentiate the Detritus." Ask students if anyone knows what the word *detritus* (pronounced de-try-tus) means. Give students a few minutes to research the answer (i.e., waste or debris of any kind).
4. Read to students the script below outlining their next PBL task:

    > The second day of shooting will involve filming the segment of the show called "Differentiate the Detritus." This is not always a fun part of the job. It can be quite sticky and often very smelly. During this segment, you and the business owners will examine every piece of trash produced by the business over the course of a week and categorize it as either *organic* waste (i.e., was once alive) or *nonorganic* waste (i.e., human made and nonbiological). Next, you will conduct research to determine if each type of waste is either *compostable* (i.e., will decompose over time), *recyclable* (i.e., can be broken down and remade into something new), or *reusable* (i.e., can be used as is, but in a new way). You are not too excited about dumpster diving, but you agree that you will do what needs to be done. After giving the producers of the show a frown, you hold your nose and jump into the trash bin!

5. Tell students that, lucky for them, they do not really have to get into a dumpster. Instead, they will be provided with Handout 6.1: Trash Investigation Inventory, which lists all of the garbage for each business.

Distribute the handout. Ask students to read the list for their business and discuss with their group any patterns or trends they see (e.g., most of the items on the list are made of plastic, etc.).

6. Next, provide each group with Handout 6.2: Differentiate the Detritus. Challenge students to complete the table, indicating whether each item is organic or inorganic, as well as compostable, recyclable, or reusable. Students may use the Internet, books from the library, periodicals, and other materials to conduct research.
7. Toward the end of the work time, debrief as a class any additional patterns or trends students have discovered.
8. Conclude the conversation by asking students to calculate the percentage of items on their list that were organic versus inorganic. Repeat with the percentage of items that were compostable, recyclable, or useable.

TEACHER'S NOTE

If students are unfamiliar with how to calculate a percentage, refer to the following website or any other credible source you prefer: https://www.mathsisfun.com/percentage.html.

9. Allow students the opportunity to add to their Need to Know Boards (Handout 2.3) at this time.
10. **Journal prompt:** Ask students to complete the following journal prompt: *Were you surprised at the results of your calculations? How do your percentages compare to those in Lesson 2?*

Name: ______________________ Date: ____________

HANDOUT 6.1

Trash Investigation Inventory

Directions: Refer to the list that corresponds to your business.

Rosalyn's Restaurant

Styrofoam plates	Paper cups	Plastic lids for cups	Plastic straws
Paper napkins and towels	Ketchup packets	Mustard packets	Mayonnaise packets
Salt/pepper packets	Plastic silverware	Cardboard boxes	Plastic milk jugs
Wax paper	Plastic bags	Empty soap bottles	Empty toilet paper rolls
Disposable gloves	Food scraps	Plastic spray bottles	Aluminum foil
Glass jars	Plastic containers	Paper receipts	Wooden stir sticks
Sugar packets	Coffee cup sleeves	Coffee creamer packets	Styrofoam coffee cups
Grease	Egg cartons	Tin cans	Old mop heads and cloth towels

Charlie's Toy Chest

Cardboard boxes	Plastic bags	Styrofoam peanuts	Wooden pallets
Paper receipts	Plastic spray bottles	Empty toilet paper rolls	Paper towels and tissues
Used stuffed animals	Used puzzles	Used action figures	Used toy cars
Used game pieces	Used wooden blocks	Used plastic blocks	Used baby dolls
Used rubber balls	Used marbles	Broken drones	Broken LEGO bricks
Tissue paper	Paper clips	Batteries	Plastic sale signs
Plastic straps	Printer cartridges	Plastic wrap	Hand sanitizer bottles
Candy wrappers	Old metal bookshelf	Rope or twine	Cigarette butts swept up from front sidewalk

Name: ______________________________ Date: ______________

HANDOUT 6.1, continued

M&B Motel

Small shampoo bottles	Bar soap wrappers	Partially used soap	Detergent bottles
Empty toilet paper rolls	Paper receipts	Plastic cups	Printer cartridges
Styrofoam coffee cups	Sugar packets	Coffee cup sleeves	Styrofoam plates
Coffee creamer packets	Wooden stir sticks	Used cloth slippers	Baby diapers
Disposable razors	Cotton balls and cotton swabs	Food wrappers	Plastic bags
Soda bottles	Paper cups	Plastic cup lids	Plastic straws
Soda cans	Food scraps	Paper towels and tissues	Plastic spray bottles
Tree limbs, grass trimmings, leaves, etc.	Cardboard boxes	Disposable gloves	Shaving cream bottles

Name: ______________________ Date: ____________

HANDOUT 6.2

Differentiate the Detritus

Directions: List each item of trash and place an "X" in the columns next to each to indicate the item's qualities.

Item	Organic	Inorganic	Compostable	Fully Recyclable	Partially Recyclable	Reusable

Name: ______________________________ Date: ______________

HANDOUT 6.2, continued

Item	Organic	Inorganic	Compostable	Fully Recyclable	Partially Recyclable	Reusable

What patterns or trends do you notice after analyzing the data?

LESSON 7

The Plastic Problem

Objectives

- Students will investigate the problems plastic poses around the globe.
- Students will research and brainstorm solutions to the problem.

Materials

- Handout 2.3: Need to Know Board
- Handout 6.2: Differentiate the Detritus
- Empty plastic bottle
- Student access to SCAMPER app (available at http://scamper.site44.com/index.html)
- Student access to Sandra Kaplan's Depth and Complexity Model (available at http://depthandcomplexity.site44.com)
- Student journals

Assessments

- Handout 2.3: Need to Know Board
- Journal prompt

Procedures

1. Review major concepts from the previous lesson (e.g., organic, nonorganic, compostable, reusable, etc.).
2. Point out to students that many of the items on Handout 6.1: Trash Investigation Inventory are made of plastic. Explain to students that the United States produces 35.7 million tons of plastic waste a year (U.S. EPA, n.d.-b).
3. Poll students to see if anyone knows what plastic is made of (i.e., traditional plastics are made of petroleum).
4. Ask students to consult their copies of Handout 6.2: Differentiate the Detritus to see if the items made of plastic on their lists are compostable (i.e., petroleum-based plastics are not).
5. Ask students to consult Handout 6.2: Differentiate the Detritus to see if the plastic items on their lists are recyclable (i.e., most plastic can be recycled, but it is too expensive to process items like plastic bags, film, etc.). Due to this fact, only 9% of plastics produced around the world are recycled (United Nations, 2018).
6. Ask students to consult Handout 6.2: Differentiate the Detritus to see if the items made of plastic on their lists are reusable (i.e., some plastic products can be reused, but more and more plastics are considered single-use plastics, like straws, gloves, and grocery bags).
7. Challenge students to see if they can remember which of the two remaining tools we still have available to us from Lesson 4 (i.e., reduce and reimagine).
8. Display a plastic bottle for students. Challenge them to work in small groups to brainstorm as many ways as they can to avoid using or buying products in plastic bottles. Give each group an opportunity to share a few of their unique ideas.
9. Next, introduce students to the SCAMPER strategy (Eberle, 1996) by explaining what each letter stands for:
   - **S**ubstitute
   - **C**ombine
   - **A**dapt

- **M**odify/minify/magnify
- **P**ut to other uses
- **E**liminate
- **R**earrange

10. Direct students to the SCAMPER app (see Materials) to see examples of each letter in the acronym.
11. Provide time for students to brainstorm and/or research ways to reimagine a plastic bottle using SCAMPER. Once again, provide an opportunity for students to share a few of their ideas with the class.
12. Direct students to Sandra Kaplan's Depth and Complexity Model (see Materials). Explain that the site includes the components of Sandra Kaplan's (2009) Depth and Complexity model. Ask them to click on the "Change Over Time" tab and read the information.

TEACHER'S NOTE

To learn more about the Depth and Complexity model, see Kaplan (2009).

13. Explain to students that almost everything changes with time, including the science of making plastics.
14. Share with students three current examples of innovations in the science of making plastics created by real environmental engineers. Three possible examples are:
    - **Edible Plastic Bags:** https://www.cnn.com/travel/article/nara-deer-plastic-bags-scli-intl-scn/index.html
    - **Plastics-to-Fuel:** https://magazine.wharton.upenn.edu/digital/saving-world-plastics-to-fuel
    - **Outdoor Furniture Made From Recycled Milk Jugs:** https://breezesta.com/sustainability

15. Ask students to predict what plastic making may look like 100 years in the future.
16. Give students time to add any new information they would like to remember to their Need to Know Boards (Handout 2.3).

17. **Journal prompt:** Ask students to complete the following journal prompt: *Some people describe experiencing plastic shaming (i.e., being made to feel guilty for using disposable, nonrecyclable plastic). Do you think plastic shaming is a good thing or a bad thing? Explain your thoughts.*

LESSON 8

A Look at the Books

Objective

- Students will calculate profits and losses for their companies using a sample general ledger spanning 5 days in time.

Materials

- Handout 2.3: Need to Know Board
- Handout 8.1: General Ledgers
- Student computer and Internet access for research
- Student journals

Assessments

- Handout 2.3: Need to Know Board
- Handout 8.1: General Ledgers
- Journal prompt

Procedures

1. Review major concepts from the previous lesson (e.g., SCAMPER, recent plastic innovations, etc.).
2. Introduce students to the next phase of the problem-based learning task by reading the following script:

   > Now that you have had a chance to get cleaned up after your dumpster-diving experience, it is time to take a close look at your company's financial records. This segment of the show is called "Look at the Books." Each group will be provided with a 5-day span of your company's general ledger. A general ledger is one way a business keeps track of all income from sales or services and expenses from purchasing supplies and paying bills. The general ledgers you will receive have missing information. You will need to work with your teammates to calculate the ending balance each day, as well as research the costs of particular items your business owners purchased. A few suggested sites for each business include:
   >
   > - **Rosalyn's Restaurant:** https://www.restaurantsupply.com, https://www.webstaurantstore.com
   > - **Charlie's Toy Chest:** https://www.alibaba.com (search "wholesale toys"), https://dir.indiamart.com (search "kids toys")
   > - **M&B Motel:** https://www.hotelsupplies-online.com, https://www.nathosp.com

3. Provide students with the remainder of the lesson time to work. Based on the needs of your students, calculators may be provided.
4. Debrief with students a few minutes before class ends.
5. Ask students to record any new information or questions on their Need to Know Boards (Handout 2.3).

6. **Journal prompt:** Ask students to complete the following journal prompt: *What surprised you the most about your company's general ledgers?*

Name: ______________________ Date: ______________

HANDOUT 8.1

General Ledgers

Account: Rosalyn's Restaurant

Account #: ______________________

Date	Description	Quantity	Debit	Credit	Current Balance
10/22	Disposable plastic utensils and paper cups	30-day supply	$		$14,938
10/22	Revenue from meals and drinks served			$975	
10/23	Revenue from meals and drinks served			$1,206	
10/24	Napkins, paper towels, toilet paper	30-day supply	$		
10/24	Revenue from meals and drinks served			$874	
10/25	Styrofoam plates and coffee cups	30-day supply	$		
10/25	Revenue from meals and drinks served			$1,008	
10/26	Coffee grounds, milk, soda canisters	14-day supply	$		
10/26	Ketchup, mustard, and mayonnaise packets	30-day supply	$		
10/26	Revenue from meals and drinks served			$791	

Name: ______________________________ Date: ______________

HANDOUT 8.1, continued

Account: Charlie's Toy Chest

Account #: ______________________________

Date	Description	Quantity	Debit	Credit	Current Balance
10/22	Revenue from new toy sales			$573	$24,105
10/23	Plastic bags and tissue paper	30-day supply	$		
10/23	Monthly electric bill		$		
10/23	Revenue from new toy sales			$1,081	
10/24	Garbage pick-up (old/broken/returned toys)		$		
10/24	Revenue from new toy sales			$792	
10/25	Action figures from China + shipping	1,000 (variety)	$		
10/25	Revenue from new toy sales			$468	
10/26	Puzzles from India + shipping	500 (variety)	$		
10/26	Revenue from new toy sales			$635	

Name: ______________________ Date: ____________

Account: M&B Motel

Account #: ______________________

Date	Description	Quantity	Debit	Credit	Current Balance
10/22	Laundry detergent, dryer sheets	30-day supply	$		$56,239
10/22	Monthly water bill		$		
10/22	Revenue from guests ($75 a room)	9 rooms filled		$	
10/23	Revenue from guests ($75 a room)	8 rooms filled		$	
10/24	Travel-sized toiletries (shampoo, conditioner, lotion, bars of soap, etc.)	30-day supply	$		
10/24	Revenue from guests ($75 a room)	12 rooms filled		$	
10/25	Revenue from guests ($75 a room)	7 rooms filled		$	
10/26	Disposable cloth slippers	30-day supply	$		
10/26	Revenue from guests ($75 a room)	5 rooms filled		$	

LESSON 9

Saving Green by Going Green

Objective

- Students will estimate the cost savings from choosing one greener alternative.

Materials

- Handout 2.3: Need to Know Board
- Handout 8.1: General Ledgers
- Shel Silverstein's poem "Sarah Cynthia Sylvia Stout"
- Highlighters
- Student journals

Assessments

- Handout 2.3: Need to Know Board
- Journal prompt

Procedures

1. Review major concepts from the previous lesson (e.g., purpose of general ledgers, how to calculate expenses, etc.).
2. Introduce the term *throwaway society* and ask students what they think it means. Define it as the overuse of disposable items.
3. Read to students the poem "Sarah Cynthia Sylvia Stout" by Shel Silverstein. Explain to students that this poem is the perfect example of why we as a society need to move away from disposable, one-use items. Ask students to estimate how much of Sarah's waste could have been reduced, reused, recycled, reimagined, or composted.
4. Ask students to reorganize themselves into their PBL groups. Direct students to reexamine their now complete general ledgers and highlight those expenses that could be reduced or eliminated if alternative greener methods were adopted.
5. Next, assign each group the following corresponding change to investigate in more depth:
   - **Rosalyn's Restaurant:** Move from disposable silverware and cups to metal and glass.
   - **Charlie's Toy Chest:** Move from buying cheap toys overseas to green toy companies in the United States.
   - **M&B Motel:** Move from small disposable toiletries to larger refillable toiletry containers.

TEACHER'S NOTE

Remind students of the suggested resources included in Lesson 8. These sites will provide credible estimates for the costs of goods and services related to that particular industry.

6. Students' investigations and calculations should conclude with an estimate of the amount of money each company would save over the course of a year if these greener alternatives were adopted. Remind students that there may be an initial investment needed to switch to greener operating procedures (e.g., purchasing metal silverware, buying refillable glass bottles for toiletries, etc.). These costs should be subtracted from the amount saved for the first year.
7. Provide time for each group to share with the class their final calculations and the processes they went through to derive them.
8. Ask students to record what they found on their Need to Know Boards (Handout 2.3).
9. **Journal prompt:** Ask students to complete the following journal prompt: *In the next lesson, we will begin researching the science behind and issues with landfills. One problem with landfills is that they release methane and carbon dioxide into the air. Some cities collect that methane and use it as an energy source. Is this an example of reducing, reusing, recycling, or reimagining? Explain your answer.*

LESSON 10

The Legacy of Landfills

Objectives

- Students will investigate the three types of landfills and the science behind decomposition.
- Students will predict how long it will take certain types of garbage to decompose.

Materials

- Handout 2.3: Need to Know Board
- Teacher/student access to "Video Field Trip - Landfill" (available at https://www.youtube.com/watch?v=mA608GJ-EzM)
- Student access to U.S. Environmental Protection Agency (available at https://www.epa.gov)
- Student journals

Assessments

- Handout 2.3: Need to Know Board
- Journal prompt

Procedures

1. Review major concepts from the previous lesson (e.g., the term *throw-away society*, the costs of using greener alternatives, etc.).
2. Remind students that everything we throw away does not magically disappear. Everything goes somewhere. Most of what we throw away in America goes into landfills. Ask students to list everything they know or think they know about landfills.
3. Take students on a virtual field trip of a landfill (see Materials).
4. Ask students to discuss whether or not things thrown in a landfill ever decompose or break down over time naturally.
5. Share the following list of materials. Ask students to predict how long they think it takes each item to decompose. When students are finished, reveal the correct answers.
   - **Banana:** 3–4 weeks
   - **Paper bag:** 1 month
   - **Cotton rag:** 5 months
   - **Wool sock:** 1 year
   - **Cigarette butt:** 2–5 years
   - **Leather coat:** 40–50 years
   - **Rubber sole of a boot:** 50–80 years
   - **Tin can (soup or vegetable can):** 80–100 years
   - **Aluminum can (soda can):** 200–500 years
   - **Plastic six-pack rings:** 450 years
   - **Plastic jug:** 1 million years
   - **Styrofoam cup:** Unknown/never
   - **Glass bottle:** Unknown/never

6. Pose the question: *Which of the items surprised you the most? Why?*
7. Display the equation shown in Figure 1. Explain to students that most things that decompose need oxygen, moisture, time, warmth, and at least one of the five items listed vertically.
8. Explain to students that scientists have conducted studies in which they find an old landfill, dig down into it, and pull out trash that has been bur-

FIGURE 1
Decomposition Equation

Mold
Fungi
Oxygen + Moisture + Time +Warmth + Bacteria = Decomposition
Insects
Worms

ied for decades (e.g., newspapers, heads of cabbage, etc.). Surprisingly, they have found that the newspapers can still be read and that the cabbage is still recognizable.

9. Ask students to answer the following question using the formula in Figure 1: *If paper is supposed to decompose in a matter of months, how can it still be readable 50 years later?* (Answer: One or more of the ingredients are missing, most often oxygen.)
10. Explain that every city has to have a solid waste management plan for disposing of waste that abides by EPA regulations. Offer students an opportunity to explore these regulations on the EPA website (see Materials).
11. Create a tree map displaying the three different types of landfills (see Figure 2).
12. Challenge students to use the EPA website or other available sources to determine what rules differentiate each of the three types:
    - **Municipal:** nonhazardous, solid waste from households
    - **Industrial:** nonhazardous, solid waste from construction sites, factories, etc.
    - **Hazardous:** toxic waste that is harmful to people and the environment
13. Ask students to determine which type of landfill the waste produced by their company would most likely go to (i.e., municipal). Provide time for groups to share and justify their answers.
14. **Journal prompt:** Ask students to respond to the following journal prompt: *What will happen when all of the landfills are full? What solutions might environmental engineers propose to solve this problem?*

FIGURE 2
Tree Map Example

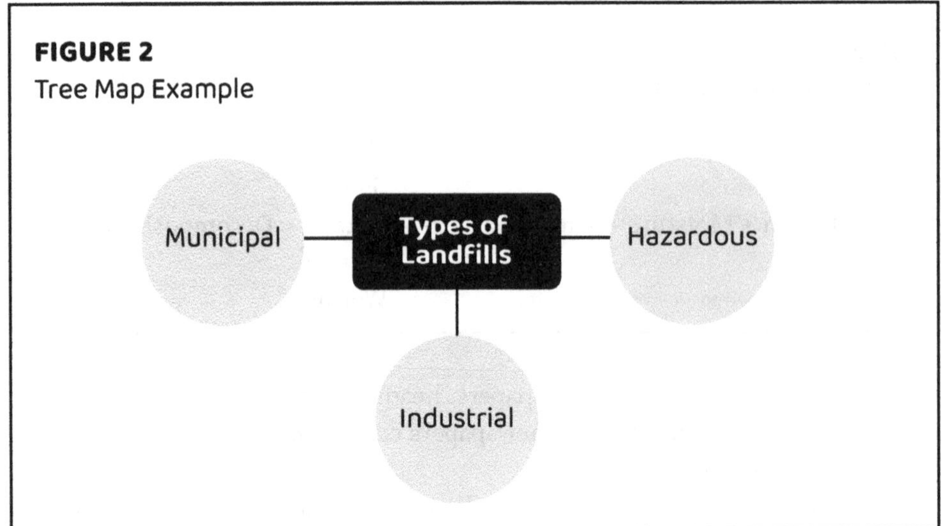

LESSON 11

Recommendation Roundup

Objectives

- Students will participate in the segment of the show called "Recommendation Roundup."
- Students will practice using a logic elimination grid.

Materials

- Handout 2.3: Need to Know Board
- Handout 4.2: 4R's Think Sheet
- Handout 11.1: *Waste Warriors* Logic Elimination Grid
- Student journals

Assessments

- Handout 2.3: Need to Know Board
- Handout 11.1: *Waste Warriors* Logic Elimination Grid
- Journal prompt

Procedures

1. Review major concepts from the previous lesson (e.g., the three types of landfills, the formula for decomposition to occur, etc.).
2. Ask students to imagine that a reporter has walked into the room and would like to ask the new cast members of *Waste Warriors* a few questions about their experience so far. Pose the following questions and ask students to talk about them in PBL groups:
   - What is it like working on a hit television show?
   - What has been your favorite part of filming your first episode?
   - What has been the most challenging?

3. Provide time for groups to share their answers with the class.
4. Explain to students that they are ready to move on to the next segment of the show entitled "Recommendation Roundup." Read the following script to students:

> Many would argue that this segment of the show is the most important. During "Recommendation Roundup," you and your teammates will generate ideas for cutting waste, evaluate the ideas using an elimination grid, and prepare a presentation for your business owners that outlines your top five recommendations. The criteria for evaluating ideas during "Recommendation Roundup" are:
>
> - the degree to which the change would reduce waste,
> - the degree to which the benefit of the change would outweigh the costs, and
> - the degree to which the change would continue to support the current business model.
>
> This phase of the show usually takes place off-screen. The only portion that is televised is the presentation to the business owners.

5. Divide students into their PBL groups. Explain to students that their first task is to brainstorm as many ideas as they can using a blank copy of Handout 4.2: 4R's Think Sheet. Students should refer back to each of the following as they work:
   - their original business plan,
   - Meet the Business Owner handouts (Handouts 5.1–5.3),
   - Handout 8.1: General Ledgers,
   - Handout 2.3: Need to Know Board, and
   - their journals.

6. Once students indicate their group has finished brainstorming ideas, challenge them to come up with at least two more. Point out that the idea here is "the more ideas, the better." Listen for students who are evaluating their own ideas or censoring others during this process. All ideas should be included and written down on the handout.
7. When it is clear that the well of ideas has run dry, distribute Handout 11.1: *Waste Warriors* Logic Elimination Grid. Use the talking points listed below to explain how to use it:

   > All ideas are to be listed vertically along the left-hand side of the table. The criteria for evaluating each idea are listed horizontally across the top. After an idea has been recorded, conduct research in order to determine the degree to which the idea meets each criteria. If the idea does not meet the criteria at all, a zero should be placed in the intersecting row and column. If the idea minimally meets the criteria (makes a small difference), a 1 should be used. If it is a solid idea and meets the criteria quite well, a 2 should be used. Lastly, if the idea fits the criteria amazingly well (makes a large difference), a 3 should be used.

8. Ask students to record the required idea from Lesson 9 in the first spot. Model for and guide students through the process of evaluating that idea using the 0–3 numbering system.
9. Provide the rest of the lesson time for students to conduct research and record information in their journals and on their Need to Know Boards (Handout 2.3).
10. **Journal prompt:** Ask students to respond to the following journal prompt: *Explain when you could use a logic elimination grid to evaluate something in your own life.*

TEACHER'S NOTE

There is more than one way to evaluate a list of ideas. A logic elimination grid is a great tool, but some students might benefit from exploring one or more of the following options. A quick search in a web browser using these phrases will provide a wealth of information and details:

- pairwise comparison,
- pass/fail,
- decision tree,
- cost/benefit analysis,
- secret ballot, and/or
- ABC analysis.

Name: ______________________________ Date: ______________

HANDOUT 11.1

Waste Warriors Logic Elimination Grid

Directions: Record all potential ideas in the first column of the table below. After conducting research, evaluate each idea using the numbering system included below.

0: Not at all 1: Small 2: Medium 3: Large

Ideas	Degree of Waste Reduction	Degree of Benefit Outweighing Cost	Degree of Business Plan Alignment	Notes
Example: Charge customers for using plastic bags.	1	3	2	

LESSON 11

LESSON 12

Researching Recommendations

Objectives

- Students will continue researching and evaluation recommendations.
- Students will begin creating a 4R's marketing campaign.

Materials

- Handout 2.3: Need to Know Board
- Handout 4.2: 4R's Think Sheet
- Handout 11.1: *Waste Warriors* Logic Elimination Grid
- Student journals

Assessments

- Handout 2.3: Need to Know Board
- Handout 11.1: *Waste Warriors* Logic Elimination Grid
- Journal prompt

Procedures

1. Review major concepts from the previous lesson (e.g., purpose of a logic elimination grid, components of the "Recommendation Roundup" segment of the show, etc.).
2. Explain to students that they will have all of this lesson to continue researching and evaluating recommendations for their business owners using Handout 11.1: *Waste Warriors* Logic Elimination Grid.
3. Before releasing students to work, explain that you have additional information that may be helpful to their brainstorming process. Share the following data:
    - **Rosalyn's Restaurant:** The average restaurant produces 100,000 pounds of waste a year, and 50% of that waste is discarded food (Dine Green, n.d.).
    - **Charlie's Toy Chest:** The average child has four toys that they have never played with (Brown, 2019). Parents admit to throwing away perfectly good toys, and 90% of all toys are made of plastic (Goldberg, 2017).
    - **M&B Motel:** The average hotel guest produces 2.2 pounds of waste each day of their stay (Helms, 2016). Much of that waste is made up of food containers, water bottles, and small toiletry bottles. The average cost to outfit a hotel room with larger reusable toiletry containers instead is only $70 a room.

4. **Anchor activity:** Introduce the following anchor activity for those who finish early. Begin by discussing the old "Give a hoot! Don't pollute!" campaign. Videos and other materials are widely available online. Explain to students that their challenge is to design a new innovative campaign designed to convince people to reduce, reuse, recycle, and reimagine waste in their daily lives. Students may create posters, videos, brochures, possible tweets, or potential social media posts, etc., for this project.

5. Remind students that the anchor activity is only to begin when and if their group completes the researching and evaluating recommendations task.
6. Release students to work.
7. Monitor, support, and ask probing questions to students as they research and evaluate their ideas.
8. A few minutes before the end of class, bring the whole group together and debrief progress made.
9. **Journal prompt:** Ask students to respond to the following journal prompt: *On a scale of one to five (one meaning badly and five meaning amazingly), how would you rate your group's collaboration today? Explain your rating.*

LESSON 13

Prepping Your Presentation

Objective

- Students will collaborate together in order to prepare a formal presentation outlining their top five ideas for going green.

Materials

- Handout 2.3: Need to Know Board
- Handout 11.1: *Waste Warriors* Logic Elimination Grid
- Highlighters
- Student journals

Assessments

- Handout 2.3: Need to Know Board
- Journal prompt

Procedures

1. Review major concepts from the previous lesson (e.g., purpose of a logic elimination grid, "Give a hoot! Don't pollute!" campaign, etc.).
2. Ask students to get out their completed logic elimination grids (Handout 11.1) and a highlighter.
3. Direct students to meet with their PBL groups and decide which of the recommendations they researched will make their final list of five. Remind students that those with the highest scores should be considered top contenders.
4. Once a decision has been reached, ask students to use a highlighter to highlight their top five recommendations.
5. Explain to students that their next task is to prepare a formal presentation for their business owners.
6. Ask students to describe the characteristics of a quality presentation. In other words, what does the presenter do or say to maximize the impact of the information they are trying to share?
7. If possible, find a video online (potentially a short TED Talk presentation), and ask students to watch and observe the speech. Direct students to talk to a partner afterward about what made the presentation successful.
8. Listen to students' responses in steps 6 and 7 above. If the following tips were not mentioned, do so now.
   - Formal presentations should be kept brief and to the point.
   - If you are presenting to a live audience, look them in the eyes. Good eye contact is essential.
   - Include data to back up the argument you are attempting to make.
   - Use technology and/or visuals carefully during your presentation. No reading from PowerPoints, too many words on a slide, etc.
   - A touch of storytelling can make the presentation memorable.
   - Analyze the audience ahead of time in order to hone your message.
   - Prepare notes to use while speaking.
   - Think through the answers to potential questions ahead of time.
   - Practice beforehand with peers.

9. Ask students to meet with their PBL groups and assign the following roles:
   - The Researcher (the person in charge of finding answers to questions online or in other reference materials)
   - The Typist/Writer (the person formulating the group's ideas into words)
   - The Visual Artist (the person formulating the group's ideas into graphs, charts, pictures)
   - The Audience Analyzer and Grammarian (the person who is responsible for thinking like an audience member and checking the writing for grammatical errors)
   - The Encourager and Project Manager (the person who keeps the group motivated, positive, on schedule, and productive)

TEACHER'S NOTE

The list of roles included here is only a sample of many possible roles a teacher could select. Check out a few additional options and modify your list according to the needs or interests of your students:

- the Motivator,
- the Discussion Leader,
- the Timekeeper,
- the Materials Manager,
- the Data Collector,
- the Quiet Captain (monitor the noise of the group as they work), and
- the Search Pilot (the one whose fingers actually touch the keyboard if sharing a computer).

10. Explain to students that the roles they have chosen are not their only responsibilities. Every person is to contribute to the presentation as a whole and help when asked. However, they will be the "go-to person" for their chosen role. Also, each person in the group must present a portion of the presentation when the time comes.

11. Provide the rest of the class period for students to work on their "Recommendation Roundup" presentations.

TEACHER'S NOTE

Telling students up front that each person must participate in the delivery of the presentation in front of the class will provide more introverted or shy students time to mentally and emotionally prepare.

12. Debrief with students a few minutes before the end of the lesson.
13. **Journal prompt:** Ask students to respond to the following journal prompt: *Many people report that public speaking is their biggest fear. How would you describe your level of comfort when speaking in front of a group?*

LESSON 14

Pitching Your Plan

Objectives

- Students will finish preparing their formal presentations.
- Students will practice presenting in front of their peers and provide constructive feedback to classmates.

Materials

- Handout 2.3: Need to Know Board
- Notes and visuals for making presentations
- 3" x 5" index cards
- Student journals

Assessments

- Handout 2.3: Need to Know Board
- Feedback cards
- Journal prompt

Procedures

1. Review major concepts from the previous lesson (e.g., characteristics of a high-quality formal presentation, who has chosen each role in the preparation of the presentations, etc.).
2. Give students another 15 minutes (if needed) to finish preparing their presentations for the class.

TEACHER'S NOTE

Taking the time to discuss the proper way to deliver and accept constructive criticism is very important. A few talking points for this discussion include:

- Disagree with ideas and not people.
- No one is perfect, and there is always room for improvement.
- Speak to others the way you would wish to be spoken to.
- Comments we give to our peers should be actionable and not simply value statements (e.g., say, "I think you could make that point a little clearer," not things like "That sounds dumb the way it is worded").

3. Bring students back together as a whole group and explain the process for presenting and providing feedback (i.e., all members of the group must speak at one point during the presentation, and the audience members will act as environmental engineers and provide feedback to each group

after the completion of each presentation). The feedback will come in the form of index cards on which the audience members have answered the following three questions:

- What did you like about the presentation and/or the top five recommendations?
- Do you believe the business owners will be swayed by the presentation? Why or why not?
- What advice, suggestions, or questions do you have for this group?

4. Ask a group to volunteer to go first. Provide time for each group to present and for the audience members to complete feedback cards.
5. Once all presentations have been made, quickly scan through the feedback cards looking for anything that may be deemed inappropriate or harshly worded.
6. Distribute the feedback cards to each group. Provide time for each group to read the feedback, conduct additional research, and/or make adjustments to their plans.
7. Encourage students to add any needed information to their Need to Know Boards (Handout 2.3).
8. **Journal prompt:** Ask students to respond to the following journal prompt: *How do you feel your presentation went today? Be specific and provide evidence.*

Lesson 14

LESSON 15

Revision for Submission

Objectives

- Students will modify their top five recommendations according to the business owner's feedback.
- Students will collaboratively choose one question to pose to the business owners.

Materials

- Handout 2.3: Need to Know Board
- Handout 11.1: *Waste Warriors* Logic Elimination Grid
- Handout 15.1: Revision for Submission
- Dice

Assessments

- Handout 2.3: Need to Know Board
- Handout 15.1: Revision for Submission
- Journal prompt

Procedures

1. Review major concepts from the previous lesson (e.g., memorable moments from student presentations, etc.).
2. Explain to students that, since the previous lesson, you were able to give each business owner an opportunity to provide feedback on students' lists of recommendations. The feedback you received was very positive; however, all three business owners asked for clarification and revisions on at least one of the ideas.
3. Direct students to retrieve their completed copies of Handout 11.1: *Waste Warriors* Logic Elimination Grid and number the highlighted ideas from 1 to 5.
4. Ask one member from each group to roll a die. The number that is rolled corresponds to the feedback that was provided:
   - **Roll a 1:** Provide more evidence for *or* replace recommendation #1.
   - **Roll a 2:** Provide more evidence for *or* replace recommendation #2.
   - **Roll a 3:** Provide more evidence for *or* replace recommendation #3.
   - **Roll a 4:** Provide more evidence for *or* replace recommendation #4.
   - **Roll a 5:** Provide more evidence for *or* replace recommendation #5.
   - **Roll a 6:** Provide more evidence for *or* replace the recommendation of your choosing.

TEACHER'S NOTE

If one or more of your teams clearly has an idea on their list that is subpar and needs major revisions, simply skip the dice activity and ask those students to revise that particular idea. Rolling the dice is fun, but the most important objective is to end up with a strong list of recommendations.

5. Distribute Handout 15.1: Revision for Submission to each group. Explain that their task today is to provide a stronger case for the idea rolled or completely abandon it altogether for a new idea. The Revision for Submission must be completed by the end of the lesson.
6. Tell students that they will have the opportunity, if needed, to ask their business owners one and only one question as they work. The group will need to come to a consensus on what that question will be.
7. Monitor and support students as they work. Answer the one question each group presents to you on behalf of the fictional business owners. Remind students to write the answer to their question on their Need to Know Boards (Handout 2.3).
8. A few minutes before the end of class, bring students together as a whole group and ask each group to share what they recorded on their Revision for Submission with the class. Collect the handout to "submit" to the business owners.
9. **Journal prompt:** Ask students to respond to the following journal prompt: *You only had one class period to complete this task. How did the added time pressure effect your ability to work?*

Name: ____________________ Date: ____________

HANDOUT 15.1

Revision for Submission

1. Who is/are your business owner(s)? (Circle one.)

   Rosalyn Charlie Sylvia and Mark

2. What was the original idea you had to modify or justify? (Write in the space below.)

3. Were you able to find additional convincing evidence to sway your business owners to accept the idea above OR did you have to research a new idea? (Place an X on the corresponding line below)

   _______ Additional Convincing Evidence Found

   _______ New Idea Proposed

4. Complete the appropriate box below.

Additional Convincing Evidence	Description of New Idea
Sources:	Sources:

LESSON 16

Roadmap to Recycling

Objectives

- Students will investigate the process by which one waste product generated from their individual businesses is recycled.
- Students will research what can and cannot be recycled in their local city.

Materials

- Handout 16.1: Roadmap to Recycling
- Student computer and Internet access for research
- Trash can
- Recycling container
- Large bag of clean, safe trash for sorting

Assessments

- Handout 16.1: Roadmap to Recycling
- Journal prompt

Procedures

1. Review major concepts from the previous lesson (e.g., revised ideas for business owners, etc.).
2. Explain to students that one of the purposes of *Waste Warriors* is to educate the viewers on the problem of waste and provide possible remedies. During the episode you are currently working on, the producers have decided to include a short segment entitled "A Behind-the-Scenes Look at a Recycling Plant."
3. As a result of this added segment, students' major task for today is to research and diagram the process by which one waste product produced by your business is recycled. Assign the following items to each PBL group:
   - **Rosalyn's Restaurant:** tin cans
   - **Charlie's Toy Chest:** cardboard boxes
   - **M&B Motel:** mini plastic toiletry bottles

TEACHER'S NOTE

Instead of assigning students one object to research, consider allowing students to choose an item listed on their Differentiate the Detritus handout (Handout 6.2).

4. Before students begin their research, explain that many towns have different processes for and regulations around what and how something is recycled. Provide students with 10 minutes to research the rules and regulations for recycling in your town.
5. Debrief what students discover as a class. Ensure that everyone is clear on what can and cannot be recycled in your city.

6. Point out that regardless of where you live, the first step at any recycling plant is to sort the trash into like groups. Take students outside with a regular trash can, a recycling bin, and a bag of clean trash. Play the following recycling relay race:
   - Divide students into 2–3 teams. Each team should form a line. Place a trash can and a recycling bin at the end of the line. Place a bag of clean garbage at the beginning of the line.
   - When you say "Begin," the person at the beginning of each line should take an item out of the bag and pass it quickly down the line. Once it reaches the person at the end of the line, they are to decide whether to put it in the recycling bin or the trash can according to your local city's recycling regulations. When finished, that person is to race to the beginning of the line, pull out another piece of trash and begin passing it down the line.
   - This process is repeated until all items have been sorted. The line that finishes correctly first is the winner.

7. Take students back inside and distribute Handout 16.1: Roadmap to Recycling. Direct students to get into their PBL groups and begin conducting research in order to fully understand each step in the recycling process for their group's waste item. Each PBL group is to create a diagram of this process using this handout.
8. Bring students back together as a whole group for a few minutes before the end of class. Ask each group to share what they discovered.
9. **Journal prompt:** Ask students to respond to the following journal prompt: *Many developed countries, like the United States and Canada, send much of their waste collected for recycling to other countries that have poor waste management plans for processing. This allows the developed countries to claim the materials were recycled even though they have no way of knowing for sure if the items were recycled or not. In fact, most of the exported waste is illegally burned or dumped when it arrives to its destination (Dell, 2020). Should this be allowed? Explain your answer.*

Name: ______________________ Date: ______________

HANDOUT 16.1

Roadmap to Recycling

Directions: Answer the two questions below *before* conducting your research. Add on to the flow map started for you below (one box for each step) *after* conducting your research.

1. Which product are you researching? (Circle one.)

   Tin cans   Cardboard boxes   Plastic toiletry bottles

2. How many steps do you estimate it will take to recycle your product? ______________

3. Complete the flow map below explaining each step in the recycling process.

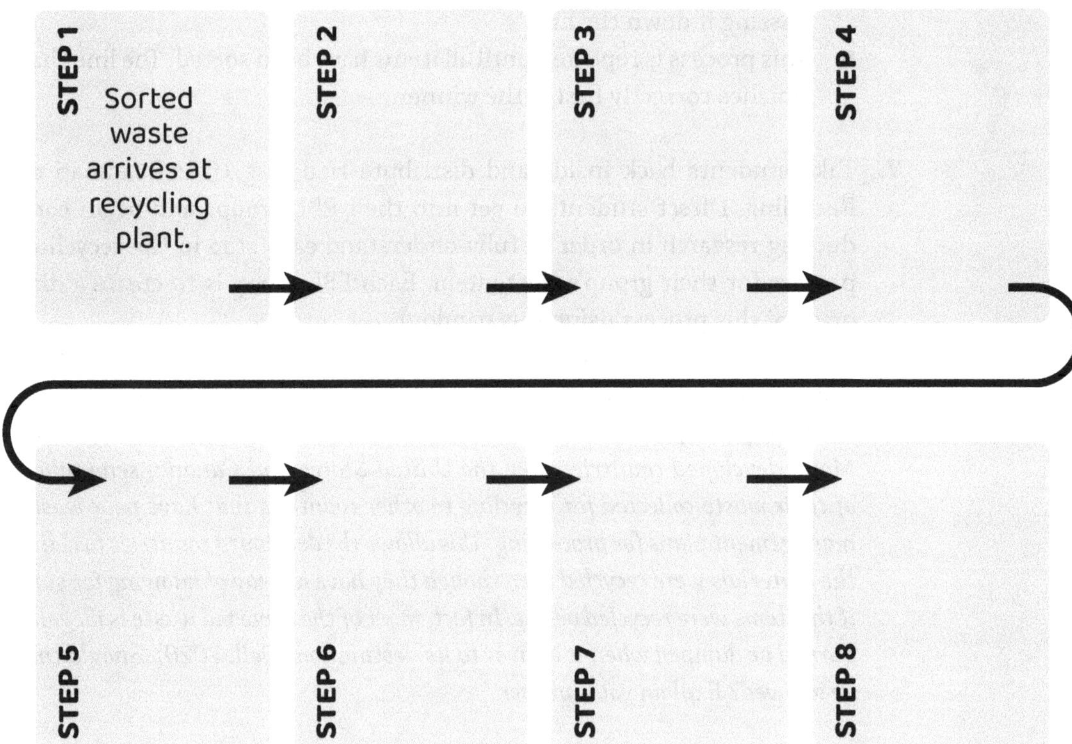

Continue adding as many additional squares as needed!

LESSON 16

LESSON 17

It's Tally Time

Objectives

- Students will participate in the "Tally Time" portion of the show.
- Students will calculate the percentage of waste reduction for their businesses using two variables.

Materials

- Handout 2.3: Need to Know Board
- Handout 17.1: Tally Time Data Tables
- Student journals

Assessments

- Handout 17.1: Tally Time Data Tables
- Journal prompt

Procedures

1. Review major concepts from the previous lesson (e.g., local ordinances on recycling, steps in recycling different objects, etc.).
2. Announce to students that you have heard back from the business owners and that congratulations are in order. Each owner has signed off on the new lists of recommendations.
3. Ask a volunteer from each group to share how their revised recommendation list changed over time.
4. Introduce the next segment of the show, "Tally Time," using the following script:

   > The producers and your business owners are very pleased with how you have performed so far in your first episode. We have now reached a crucial moment in the arch of the show—"Tally Time." In this segment of the show, calculations are made and scores are given in order to rank each team. The rankings will be determined by examining two key measures: (a) the percentage of decrease in the overall net volume of waste, and (b) the financial implications of the measures taken to reduce the waste. The most efficient team of "Waste Warriors" will have a significant advantage in the bonus round that will follow. When you are ready to proceed, signal the producers and they will ready the set for filming.

5. Share with students how the volume of waste will be calculated using the following explanation:

   > We will refer to the percentage of the decrease in the volume of waste as WD (Waste Diversion Rate). It can be calculated in various ways. Some companies weigh their trash during a particular period of time (e.g., 2 weeks) prior to any waste reduction initiatives being implemented and then compare that number to the weight of the garbage

after reduction programs have been implemented. Other companies divide the weight of the items sorted for recycling by the weight of *all* trash (recycled plus items going to the landfill). Regardless of the method chosen, two variables are needed. Due to the fact we are working with imaginary waste (and it is therefore impossible to weigh it), we are not going to work with weight. Instead, we are going to estimate the overall number of a limited list of items that will no longer end up in the trash can.

6. Distribute Handout 17.1: Tally Time Data Tables to each group. Discuss the information it contains. Ask students to complete the data table corresponding to their business and then stop.

TEACHER'S NOTE

Based on the needs of your students, determine who might need additional accommodations. Possible options include providing a calculator, reviewing how to multiply or divide, discussing the relationship between decimals and percentages, etc.

7. When everyone has finished, bring students together as a whole group, debrief the process, and ask students to share their final Waste Diversion Rates.
8. Direct students' attention to the end of the Tally Time Data Tables handout. Discuss the directions and provide time for students to work.
9. Ask students *not* to share the results of the financial impact of their five recommendations with anyone except you. Instruct students to record the information on a fresh page in their journal so that they can easily access it.
10. Collect all completed handouts and debrief the process of calculating the financial impact, but *not* the results.
11. **Journal prompt:** Ask students to respond to the following journal prompt: *Which of your five recommendations had the largest impact? How do you know?*

Name: ____ Date: ____________________

HANDOUT 17.1

Tally Time Data Tables

Directions: Use your business's table to calculate your waste diversion rate (WD) over a 2-week period. Then, follow the directions outlined at the end.

Rosalyn's Restaurant

(Assume 100 Customers Served Per Day)

<table>
<tr><th>BEFORE Waste Warriors</th><th>AFTER Waste Warriors</th><td rowspan="8">WD
(Waste Diversion Rate)

(# Before – # After) / # Before

________ × 100 = ________ %</td></tr>
<tr><td>1,083 pounds of food waste
(Count each pound as 1 item)</td><td></td></tr>
<tr><td>968 plastic utensils</td><td></td></tr>
<tr><td>1,257 plastic cups</td><td></td></tr>
<tr><td>182 tin cans</td><td></td></tr>
<tr><td>2,207 used ketchup & mustard packets</td><td></td></tr>
<tr><td>You choose an item:</td><td></td></tr>
<tr><td>Total # of Items Thrown Away:</td><td>Total # of Items Thrown Away:</td></tr>
</table>

LESSON 17

Name: ______________________________ Date: ______________

Charlie's Toy Chest

(Assume 50 Customers Visit the Store Each Day)

BEFORE *Waste Warriors*	**AFTER *Waste Warriors***	
94 cardboard boxes of various sizes		
440 pounds of wooden pallets *(Count each pound as 1 item)*		
2,500 Styrofoam peanuts		
Plastic wrap from 285 toys		**WD (Waste Diversion Rate)** (# Before – # After) / # Before ________ × 100 = ________ %
60 broken toys (from insurance policy program)		
You choose an item:		
Total # of Items Thrown Away:	Total # of Items Thrown Away:	

Name: ______________________________ Date: ______________

M&B Motel

(Assume 9 rooms are full each day, equaling 25 total guests)

BEFORE *Waste Warriors*	AFTER *Waste Warriors*	
1,856 small plastic toiletry containers		
428 water bottles		
354 *pairs* of disposable cloth slippers (354 × 2 = 708 slippers)		**WD (Waste Diversion Rate)** (# Before – # After) / # Before ________ × 100 = ________ %
475 Styrofoam coffee cups		
602 pounds of yard trimmings *(Count each pound as 1 item)*		
You choose an item:		
Total # of Items Thrown Away:	Total # of Items Thrown Away:	

How to Calculate the Financial Impact of Your "Big Five"

1. Look at column one in the table associated with your business.
2. Estimate the cost of each item on your list using online stores.
3. Total the expenditures BEFORE *Waste Warriors* and record this number on the next page.
4. Look at column two in the table associated with your business.

Name: ______________________________ Date: ______________

5. Estimate the cost of each item on your list using online stores (do not factor in one-time costs like buying larger reusable toiletry containers or purchasing real metal silverware this time).
6. Total the expenditures AFTER *Waste Warriors* and record this number in the chart below.
7. Subtract the TOTAL AFTER from the TOTAL BEFORE and report this value in the chart below.

Financial Impact of Changes

Total Expenditures **BEFORE** *Waste Warriors*: ______________________________

Total Expenditures **AFTER** *Waste Warriors* : ______________________________

Total Overall Savings: ______________________________

LESSON 18

Recalibrating to Recycle Fest

Objectives

- Students will identify which element of SCAMPER and/or which of the 4R's were used after completing an art project using trash.
- Students will begin the process of creating their bonus round product to sell at Recycle Fest.

Materials

- Handout 6.1: Trash Investigation Inventory
- Handout 17.1: Tally Time Data Tables
- Bubble wrap
- Paint and brushes

- Paper scraps (potentially leftover construction paper from the art teacher or a previous activity)
- Sheets of paper
- Student journals

Assessments

- Crumbled Creatures, final envelops, or bubble wrap prints
- Journal prompt

Procedures

1. Review major concepts from the previous lesson (e.g., how to calculate WD rate, etc.).
2. Calculate the "Tally Time" scores for each team using the procedures described below:
    - Compare the WD rate for each team.
    - Assign the team with the highest percentile 3 points. Assign the second highest team 2 points. Assign the lowest scoring team 1 point.
    - Compare the total overall savings in dollars for each team.
    - Assign the team with the highest amount saved 3 points. Assign the second highest team 2 points. Assign the lowest amount saved 1 point.
    - Add the scores for WD rate and total savings together for each team.
    - The team with the highest number of points is now in first place. (In case of a tie, the team with the highest WD rate should be granted the win.)

3. Explain to students that they will learn about the bonus round today. As mentioned before, the team who won the "Tally Time" round will have an advantage. Read the following script:

    > Congratulations! You've made it to the bonus round. I can imagine you are anxious to find out what the producers have in store for you. Well, here goes! After consulting with the local mayor and city council, it has been decided that this year's Broccoli Festival will receive a new theme. This year it will morph into the first ever Recycle Fest, and will take place in one week's time. Each business will be

provided with a booth at no expense to the owner. Your task is to create one product to sell to the public at your booth that is made entirely from the waste produced from your own business. The team who makes the most money selling their creative product will be declared the winner of the bonus round. However, the team who won the "Tally Time" segment of the show will have a significant advantage. That team can use the waste they produce as well as one item of garbage from each of the other two rival teams' waste lists. Be creative, remember your 4R's, and have fun!

4. Ask students if they have any questions about the directions for the task.
5. Share with students the following three examples of turning trash into a usable product or piece of art:
   - **Crumpled Creations:** https://mosswoodconnections.com/activity/crumpled-creations-2
   - **Bubble Wrap Printing:** https://www.artycraftykids.com/art/bubble-wrap-printing
   - **Make an Envelope:** https://www.wikihow.com/Make-an-Envelope

6. Challenge students to complete one of the three projects. When students are finished, ask them to identify which of the 4R's and/or which portion of the SCAMPER strategy they used to create their project.
7. Divide students into their PBL groups and give them the rest of the lesson time to brainstorm and research ideas. Potential resources to help may include one or more of the following:
   - *Zero Waste: Simple Life Hacks to Drastically Reduce Your Trash* by Shia Su
   - *Garbage: Investigate What Happens When You Throw It Out* by Donna Latham
   - *TIME Sustainability: The Practical, Sustainable Life*

8. A few minutes before class ends, bring students together as a class. Ask groups to share a potential idea they are exploring.
9. Inform students that they will have time during the next lesson to refine ideas and research alternatives.
10. **Journal prompt:** Ask students to respond to the following journal prompt: *The entertainment and food committees for Recycle Fest are looking for ideas. In your opinion, what type of entertainment and food should be offered during the festival?*

LESSON 19

Product Proposals

Objective

- Students will continue the process of creating their bonus round product to sell at Recycle Fest.

Materials

- Handout 19.1: Recycle Fest Materials and Instructions List
- Three pieces of waste (one from each business's trash inventory list)
- Student journals

Assessments

- Handout 19.1: Recycle Fest Materials and Instructions List
- Journal prompt

Procedures

1. Review major concepts from the previous lesson (e.g., the details of the bonus round, etc.).
2. Explain to students that they will have most of this lesson time to finalize an idea for their product. However, before they begin working independently, you have created a warm-up activity to help get their creative juices flowing:
   - Direct students to sit in a circle.
   - Show students one of the three objects you have brought with you today (one item from each business's inventory list).
   - Share an idea that you, as the teacher, have for turning that object into a usable product or piece of art.
   - Pass it to the person beside you and ask that student to share a different idea.
   - Continue around the circle until everyone has had a chance to share an idea.
   - Repeat the process with the second and third pieces of waste.

TEACHER'S NOTE

Talk to students about the brainstorming strategy known as piggybacking. This means to take someone else's idea, add to it, and make it slightly different. Contrast piggybacking with copying an idea so that students have a clear understanding of the differences.

3. Distribute Handout 19.1: Recycle Fest Materials and Instructions List. Tell students that this must be filled out before the end of the lesson

because students will be creating a sample prototype of the product during the next lesson. Remind students that piggybacking on ideas generated during the circle activity is perfectly acceptable.

4. Allow students to begin working with their groups to finalize a product idea.
5. Monitor and ask students questions as they work.
6. Regroup as a whole group a few minutes before the class ends. Ask groups to share the highlights of their completed plan.

TEACHER'S NOTE

Instead of trying to provide the materials each group needs to create their prototype during the next class lesson, poll students and see who has what items they are willing to donate to the cause.

7. **Journal prompt:** Ask students to respond to the following journal prompt: *Explain the differences between piggybacking and copying someone. In your opinion, should credit be given to the person whose idea was piggybacked off of?*

Name: ______________________________ Date: ______________

HANDOUT 19.1

Recycle Fest Materials and Instructions List

Directions: Please answer the following questions regarding your product for Recycle Fest.

1. What will you call your product?

2. What is the purpose of your product?

3. How much will you charge for your product?

4. What materials will you need to make this product?
   - Your recycled item or items:

   - Additional materials you will need:

5. Before moving on to Question 6, use a highlighter to highlight any of the materials listed above that you do NOT have at home or are NOT readily available in this classroom.

6. Describe the steps needed to create your product on the next page. Use the back of this handout if you need more space.

Name: ______________________________ Date: ______________

HANDOUT 19.1, continued

Step 1:

Step 2:

Step 3:

LESSON 19

Prototype Preparation

Objectives

- Students will create a prototype of their Recycle Fest product.
- Students will begin researching a favorite real-world company or business of their choosing and determine its level of "greenness" to date.

Materials

- Materials listed on Handout 19.1: Recycle Fest Materials and Instructions List
- Handout 20.1: The Greenness Gauge
- Student computer and Internet access for research
- Student journals
- Various art supplies

Assessments

- Handout 20.1: The Greenness Gauge
- Journal prompt

Procedures

1. Review major concepts from the previous lesson (e.g., the details of the bonus round, etc.).
2. Explain to students that their goal is to make the first prototype of their Recycle Fest product.
3. **Anchor activity:** Before they begin working, introduce students to an anchor activity that they are to begin working on if they finish early. In short, their task over the next few lessons is to choose a company or business that they personally admire or frequently purchase from (e.g., Disney, Nike, McDonald's, PlayStation, etc.) and collect evidence as to its current level of environmental responsibility (i.e., level of greenness).

TEACHER'S NOTE

Introduce to students organizations or programs designed to evaluate the environmental impact of products on the market. Encourage students to take a few minutes to acquaint themselves with a few, such as:

- Energy Star,
- Green Seal Certification,
- USDA Organic,
- Leadership in Energy and Environmental Design (LEED) Certification, and
- Animal Welfare Approved Certification.

4. Distribute Handout 20.1: The Greenness Gauge to each student. Read and discuss the directions on the handout as a class.

5. Provide the remainder of the lesson time for students to build their prototypes and begin working on the anchor activity.
6. Monitor and support students as they work.
7. A few minutes before class ends, as a whole group, debrief the experience of creating the prototype thus far. Explain that students will have one more class period to finalize their product.
8. **Journal prompt:** Ask students to respond to the following journal prompt: *If your family was a company, how would it score on the greenness gauge? Provide reasoning for your score.*

Name: ______________________________ Date: ______________

HANDOUT 20.1

The Greenness Gauge

Directions: Choose a company whose products you enjoy buying. Gather evidence using multiple sources as to how environmentally friendly your chosen company is. Use the Greenness Gauge on the next page to give it a grade and brainstorm two changes the company could make in order to improve.

1. The company I will research is:

2. What do you like most about this company?

3. Record your findings about the company's environmental record in the chart below:

Name of Source	Findings	Date of Article	Can You Confirm the Information Using Multiple Sources?
			YES or **NO** If so, where?
			YES or **NO** If so, where?
			YES or **NO** If so, where?

LESSON 20

Name: ______________________ Date: ______________

HANDOUT 20.1, continued

4. A gauge is an instrument used to measure the amount of something. Study the Greenness Gauge below. If you had to rate the company you researched using this gauge, how would it score?

Dark Gray (A)	▶ Highly environmentally friendly ▶ Evidence was abundant and/or proved the company actively seeks to improve the environment, not just reduce their own impact
Gray (B)	▶ Solidly environmentally friendly ▶ Evidence showed the company is taking steps to reduce their environmental impact now
Light Gray (C to D)	▶ Mildly environmentally friendly ▶ Evidence was sparse and/or future plans are being made to reduce environmental impact
White (F)	▶ NOT environmentally friendly ▶ Evidence proved the company knowingly hurt the environment

The grade you would give this company is: ______________________

5. Explain your rationale.

6. What are two things the company could do to improve? Be specific!

7. Were you surprised by the results of your research? Why or why not?

LESSON 20

LESSON 21

Prototype Pros and Cons

Objectives

- Students will finalize and demonstrate their prototype.
- Students will continue researching a favorite real-world company or business in order to determine its level of "greenness" to date.

Materials

- Handout 19.1: Recycle Fest Materials and Instructions List
- Handout 20.1: The Greenness Gauge
- Handout 21.1: Prototype Pros and Cons
- Completed or partially completed prototypes
- Student journals

Assessments

- Handout 20.1: The Greenness Gauge
- Handout 21.1: Prototype Pros and Cons
- Final prototypes
- Journal prompt

Procedures

1. Review major events from the previous lesson.
2. Provide the first half of the lesson time for students to perfect their prototypes and/or work on the greenness gauge anchor activity.
3. Monitor and support students as they work.
4. Approximately halfway through the class period, bring students back together as a whole group. Explain that each group will now discuss and demonstrate their prototypes for the rest of the class. The audience members will complete a short feedback form after each presentation.
5. Distribute Handout 21.1: Prototype Pros and Cons to each student and explain how to use it. Note that each student will need multiple copies of the review sheet (one per presentation).
6. After the presentations, collect Handout 21.1 and complete the following tasks *before* handing them back to the appropriate team of students:
   - quickly scan comments to check for the appropriateness of comments, and
   - add and record each group's scores for Question 4 (but do not reveal the total to students yet).

7. Provide a few minutes for each group to read their feedback and discuss whether or not any changes are needed to the presentation, the prototype, and/or the cost.

TEACHER'S NOTE

Encourage students to pay special attention to the feedback they were given about the cost of their item. This will be a very important component in the calculations leading to a winner of the bonus round.

8. Collect Handout 21.1: Prototype Pros and Cons Review Sheet once again for use during the next class period.
9. **Journal prompt:** Ask students to respond to the following journal prompt: *Which of the prototypes was your favorite? Please explain why.*

Name: ______________________________ Date: ______________

HANDOUT 21.1

Prototype Pros and Cons

Directions: Please answer each of the questions below while reflecting on your classmates' presentations. Remember to be kind and treat others the way you would want to be treated.

1. Prototype description and purpose:

2. How many different recyclable products were used?

3. On a scale of 1 to 5, how creative was the product? (1 = not creative/ 5 = extremely creative)

   1 2 3 4 5

4. How likely would you be to purchase this product? (1 = not likely/ 5 = most definitely)

   1 2 3 4 5

5. How much would you be willing to pay for this item?

6. How could this product be improved?

7. What did you like best about the product?

8. Additional comments:

LESSON 22

Granting Greenness Grades

Objectives

- Students will calculate total sales from Recycle Fest.
- Students will finish researching a favorite real-world company or business in order to determine its level of "greenness" to date.

Materials

- Handout 20.1: The Greenness Gauge
- Handout 21.1: Prototype Pros and Cons Review Sheet
- Total scores for Question 4 on Handout 21.1: Prototype Pros and Cons
- Student journals

Assessments

- Handout 20.1: The Greenness Gauge
- Total sales calculations
- Journal prompt

Procedures

1. Review major events from the previous lesson.
2. Explain to students that the end of production on the first episode of *Waste Warriors* is drawing to a conclusion. Today they will calculate their total sales from Recycle Fest. However, a final winner will not be declared until the next lesson.
3. Guide students through the following procedure to determine their total sales:
   - Students should add the scores they were given by their classmates on Question 4 (excluding anyone from their own groups) on Handout 21.1: Prototype Pros and Cons Review Sheet. Verify this number for students using the totals recorded during the last class period.
   - Students should multiply this number by their final revised price listed on Handout 19.1: Recycle Fest Materials and Instructions List.
   - Students should double-check their calculations for accuracy.

   Example:
     - Individual scores from classmates on Question 4: 4, 1, 5, 4, 2, 3, 2, 4, 4, 3, 5, 4, 5, 3
     - Total of scores: 49
     - Final agreed-upon cost: $5.00
     - Multiply total score by cost: 49 × $5.00 = $245.00

4. Ask groups to share their final profits from Recycle Fest with the whole class. Award the group with the highest profit levels 3 points. Award the second highest group 2 points. Award the group with the lowest total profits 1 point.
5. Provide students a few minutes to reflect on the process and determine how they might improve on their product or pricing structure in the future.
6. Challenge students to complete the greenness gauge anchor activity by concluding all remaining research on the company of their choosing and

determining a final "greenness" grade for their chosen company by the end of the lesson.

7. Monitor and support students as they work. If a student finishes early, ask them to ponder the following question: Imagine you have the power to enact a new piece of legislation aimed at reducing waste and improving the environment. What would it be, and what type of an impact would it have?
8. A few minutes before the end of the lesson, debrief the lesson as a whole group.
9. **Journal prompt:** Ask students to respond to the following journal prompt: *Which business do you think will win the Waste Warriors competition? Why?*

Consuming Carefully and Consciously

Objectives

- Students will explore the problem of overconsumption.
- Students will disclose and provide justification for their greenness evaluations.

Materials

- Handout 20.1: The Greenness Gauge
- Student journals

Assessments

- Handout 20.1: The Greenness Gauge
- Journal prompt

Procedures

1. Review major events from the previous lesson.
2. Remind students that today they will share their greenness gauge evaluations from the anchor activity and learn which company is the winner of the first episode of *Waste Warriors*.
3. Before moving forward, share the following quote from Gandhi with students and ask them to discuss what it means with a partner: "There is enough in the world for everyone's need; there is not enough for everyone's greed."
4. Provide a chance for students to share their thoughts.
5. Explain to students that humans must consume water, air, food, etc., in order to stay alive. And, as humans, we enjoy purchasing things we like (but do not necessarily need), such as toys, jewelry, junk food, vacations, etc.
6. Ask students to share with the class how they would categorize the products or services the company they researched during the greenness gauge anchor activity produces: *want* or *need*.
7. Define the term *overconsumption* for students as a problem that arises when consumption becomes out of control and priorities are not aligned.
8. Provide students with the examples in Figure 3 and ask students to discuss their thoughts with a partner.

TEACHER'S NOTE

The habit of saving one's ideas is one of Sandra Kaplan's Habits of a Scholar (Kaplan, 2012). A few of the other habits include curiosity, preparation, practice, thirst for knowledge, goal setting, striving for excellence, perseverance, and intellectual risk-taking. Look for opportunities to reinforce these valuable habits whenever possible.

FIGURE 3
Products We Spend Money On

Products We Spend Money On	Annual Expenditure	Social or Economic Goal We Could Have Spent Money On	Additional Annual Investment Needed to Achieve Goal
Perfumes	$15 billion	Universal literacy	$5 billion
Ocean cruises	$14 billion	Clean drinking water for all	$10 billion
Ice cream	$11 billion in Europe alone	Immunizing every child	$1.3 billion

9. Ask students to brainstorm and record in their journals ways in which we could decrease the chances that overconsumption will occur.
10. Explain to students that they will look into the problem of overconsumption a little more in the next lesson. Until then, students should save their ideas to share during the next class period.
11. Provide the remainder of the lesson time for students to present the results of their greenness gauge anchor activities.
12. **Journal prompt:** Ask students to respond to the following journal prompt: *List as many words as you can think of that mean the opposite of* greedy *and/ or* overconsumption *(e.g.,* frugal, giving, generous, *etc.).*

LESSON 24

Mapping the Materials Economy

Objectives

- Students will sequence the stages in the materials economy.
- Students will analyze one product available on the market today and learn about its life cycle.

Materials

- Handout 24.1: Map the Materials Economy
- Student computer and Internet access for research
- Sticky notes (five per small group of students)
- Student journals

Assessments

- Handout 24.1: Map the Materials Economy
- Journal prompt

Procedures

1. Review the concept of overconsumption introduced during the previous lesson.
2. Explain to students that during this lesson, as promised, they will explore this issue and its implications for waste reduction in more depth.
3. Provide each small group of students five sticky notes.
4. Ask students to write each of the following terms on a sticky note:
   - Consumption
   - Production
   - Disposal
   - Extraction
   - Distribution

5. Explain to students that the five terms they wrote down make up the five stages in the life cycle of any product we purchase. Give students 5–10 minutes to record the definition of each term in their journals and then place the sticky notes in the order in which they believe they occur.
6. Check and verify the accuracy of each group's sticky notes (i.e., extraction, production, distribution, consumption, disposal).
7. Distribute Handout 24.1: Map the Materials Economy and explain to students that the five stages they just listed make up what is known as the materials economy.
8. Review the directions on the handout and provide time for students to work.
9. Monitor and support students throughout the process.
10. A few minutes before class ends, as a whole group, debrief the progress students have made thus far.
11. **Journal prompt:** Ask students to respond to the following journal prompt: *Which of the five stages in the materials economy do you believe does the most environmental damage? Why?*

Name: ______________________ Date: ______________

HANDOUT 24.1

Map the Materials Economy

Directions: Choose a product you have purchased in the past or would like to buy in the future. Research the details of each stage in that product's life cycle.

1. What is the name of the product you are researching?

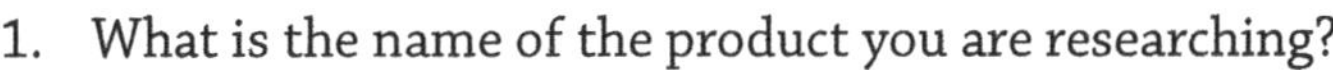

2. Who makes the product?

3. How much does it cost (in dollars)?

4. How long do you think it will last (in years)?

5. Would most people consider it a: (Circle one.)

   Want Need

6. Before doing any research, on a scale of 1 (not at all) to 5 (very much so), how harmful do you think this product is to the environment during all stages of its life cycle? (Circle one.)

   1 2 3 4 5

Name: ______________________________ Date: ______________

HANDOUT 24.1, continued

7. Conduct research in order to complete the table below:

Stage	Details	Source
Extraction	*What natural resources are used to make this product? Where are they found? How are they extracted?*	
Production	*What processes are used to create this product? What forms of energy are consumed in the production?*	
Distribution	*Where is it made? How is it shipped to customers around the world? What packaging is used?*	
Consumption	*How long does this product last? Is it durable, long-lasting, and a good investment over time?*	
Disposal	*How is this product typically disposed of? Can it be recycled, composted, reimagined, etc.?*	

8. Which of your findings surprise you? List and explain below:

9. Now, after finishing your research, rate again how harmful your product is to the environment on a scale of 1 (not at all) to 5 (very much so). (Circle one.)

1 2 3 4 5

10. What changes could be made to the extraction, production, distribution, consumption, or disposal of your product to decrease its impact on the environment?

LESSON 25

Provisional Placement in Post Production

Objectives

- Students will receive provisional rankings for the *Waste Warriors* competition.
- Students will choose a project from various options to improve their overall ranking.

Materials

- Handout 24.1: Map the Materials Economy
- Handout 25.1: Provisional Score Form
- Handout 25.2: Erase the Waste Choice Board
- Student journals

Assessments

- Handout 24.1: Map the Materials Economy
- Handout 25.1: Provisional Score Form
- Journal prompt

Procedures

1. Review the components of the materials economy with the class.
2. Provide a few minutes for students to finish Handout 24.1: Map the Materials Economy.
3. Bring students together as a whole group, and ask each student to share a short synopsis of what they discovered about the product they researched during the last class period.
4. Divide students into their PBL groups. Ask students the following question: *In light of what you just learned about the materials economy, what changes would you make to the recommendations you made for your assigned business (i.e., Rosalyn's Restaurant, Charlie's Toy Chest, M&B Motel)?*
5. Share with students the following update on the *Waste Warriors* competition:

> The producers of the show wish to thank you for participating as a cast member on your first episode of *Waste Warriors*. They also feel that if your work during the last few weeks is any indication of your true work ethic and waste elimination skills, they would like to happily extend an invitation for you to continue on as a reoccurring cast member. Having said that, however, the producers wanted to remind you that only one team can win the actual competition. The overall winner of your first episode will not be announced today though because the producers want to give your team an opportunity to view your score and potentially work toward improving it. You may see your team's data but no one else's.

6. Ask each team if they would like to see how they have scored. If they would like to see their data, complete the form provided on Handout 25.1: Provisional Score Form using their scores from pages 108 and 128. Instruct each team to keep their data strictly confidential.

7. After students have had a chance to see their data, point out the word *provisional* on the score reporting form and ask what it means (i.e., existing for the present; will possibly change later). Relate this word to the concept of change over time.
8. Explain to students that they will have one more opportunity to add to their point totals. Distribute Handout 25.2: Erase the Waste Choice Board and discuss each option along with the corresponding point totals.
9. Provide time for students to talk with their teammates and choose a course of action.

TEACHER'S NOTE

Students do *not* have the option of passing on this opportunity. They do, however, have the choice between a project worth one point, a project worth two points, or propose a topic of their own worth three points.

10. Give students all remaining class time to begin working on their chosen project.
11. **Journal prompt:** Ask students to respond to the following journal prompt: *How can you extend the life of something you have in your room at home right now?*

Name: ______________________________ Date: ______________

HANDOUT 25.1

Provisional Score Form

Name of Business: ______________________________

Part A

Waste Diversion Rate Score: (Circle one.)

1 2 3

Part B

Financial Impact Score: (Circle one.)

1 2 3

Part C

Bonus Round Score: (Circle one.)

1 2 3

Total Points (Parts A + B + C) =

Name: ______________________________ Date: ______________

HANDOUT 25.2

Erase the Waste Choice Board

Directions: Choose and complete one of the projects listed below. If your completed project meets the agreed-upon standards of quality, an additional point or points will be added to your total score.

Possible Points: 1 Design a new environmentally friendly package to ship a large tuba. It usually comes packed in one large box full of Styrofoam and plastic.	**Possible Points: 1** A gyre is a circular pattern of currents that form in the ocean. According to scientists, there is a large gyre containing thousands of miles worth of garbage in the Pacific Ocean. Pinpoint its location on a map and suggest three ways of cleaning it up.	**Possible Points: 2** Imagine you inherited an old home. Now, imagine the landfill in your town is closed. How would you empty the house in an eco-friendly way?
Possible Points: 1 During the Middle Ages in Europe, waste became a huge problem and led to what is known as the Black Death. Determine how waste became a trigger for thousands of deaths and then compare how Europe's waste removal systems have changed over time. Present your findings in a creative way.	**Possible Points: 1 or 2 or 3** Negotiate an idea of your own with the teacher.	**Possible Points: 2** Choose a room in your house (e.g., bathroom, kitchen, living room) and create a brochure that describes 10 ways to green up that space. Make sure to provide a justification for why the reader should change their current practices and take your advice.

Name: ______________________ Date: ______________

HANDOUT 25.2, continued

Possible Points: 1	**Possible Points: 2**	**Possible Points: 2**
Henry David Thoreau (1817–1862) was a famous American naturalist and poet who wrote about living sustainably and peacefully. He even built his own house out of discarded materials. Many summarize his philosophy of life as "Simplify, simplify." Read more about Thoreau's life on Walden Pond and record five ways you could simplify your own life and live more sustainably.	One of the most famous environmentalists alive today is teenager Greta Thunberg. She was named *Time*'s Person of the Year in 2019 and even spoke in front of the United Nations to leaders from around the globe. Imagine you are going to give a speech in front of the United Nations about waste reduction and sustainability. Write a first draft of your 10-minute speech and record a video of your group delivering it.	Art can capture people's attention while making a strong statement at the same time. For example, view the artwork titled Coming Soon: Quail Valley Condos (https://www.charleyharper.com/coming-soon-quail-valley-condos.html). Design your own piece of art (e.g., sculpture, painting, etc.) that has an environmental message, give it a captivating title, and write a justification for why it should win the Environmental Art Prize of the Year award.

LESSON 26

Choice Board Challenge

Part A

Objectives

- Students will solve a brainteaser.
- Students will continue working on Handout 25.2: Erase the Waste Choice Board.

Materials

- Handout 25.2: Erase the Waste Choice Board
- Handout 26.1: Brainteaser A
- Student journals

Assessment

- Journal prompt

Procedures

1. Review the events from the previous lesson.
2. Show students Handout 26.1: Brainteaser A and ask them to solve it with a partner.
3. Explain that the answer is climate change.
4. **Anchor activity:** Tell students that their anchor activity today, if they finish working on their choice board activity before the end of the lesson, is to talk with their PBL groups about what waste and garbage have to do with climate change.
5. Ask students if they have any questions about their choice board assignment.
6. Provide the rest of the class period for students to work.
7. Monitor and support students as they collaborate to finish their projects.
8. A few minutes before the class period ends, bring students back together as a whole group and debrief progress made.
9. **Journal prompt:** Ask students to respond to the following journal prompt: *How could you apply the 4R's to the use of energy (e.g., electricity, gasoline, propane) and/or methods of transportation?*

Name: ______________________ Date: ______________

HANDOUT 26.1

Brainteaser A

What is this two-word phrase?

LESSON 26

LESSON 27

Choice Board Challenge

Part B

Objectives

- Students will solve a brainteaser.
- Students will continue working on Handout 25.2: Erase the Waste Choice Board.

Materials

- Handout 25.2: Erase the Waste Choice Board
- Handout 27.1: Brainteaser B
- Student journals

Assessment

- Journal prompt

Procedures

1. Review the events from the previous lesson.
2. Show students Handout 27.1: Brainteaser B and ask them to solve it with a partner.
3. Explain that the answer is repair.
4. **Anchor activity:** Tell students that their anchor activity today, if they finish working on their choice board activity before the end of class, is to talk with their PBL groups about whether or not *repair* should be added to the list of R's (i.e., reduce, reuse, recycle, reimagine).
5. Ask students if they have any questions about their choice board assignment.
6. Provide the rest of the class period for students to work.
7. Monitor and support students as they collaborate to finish their projects.
8. A few minutes before the class period ends, bring students back together as a whole group and debrief progress made.
9. Explain that the last day to finish their choice board project is tomorrow.
10. **Journal prompt:** Ask students to respond to the following journal prompt: *Repairing something that is broken will most definitely extend its life. List three sources you could use in order to learn how to repair something.*

Name: ______________________ Date: ______________

HANDOUT 27.1

Brainteaser B

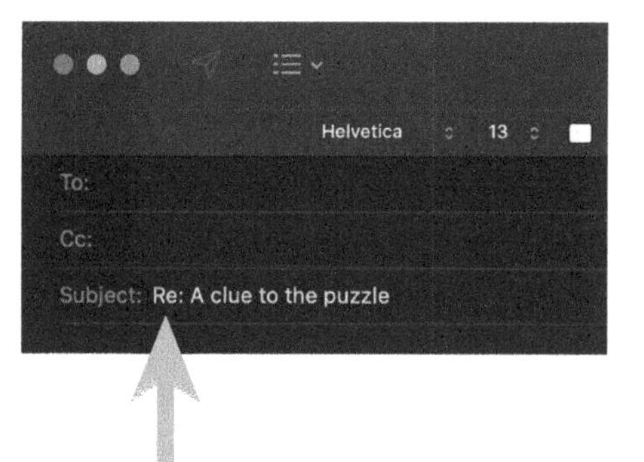

+

LESSON 27

LESSON 28

Choice Board Challenge

Part C

Objectives

- Students will solve a brainteaser.
- Students will finish Handout 25.2: Erase the Waste Choice Board.

Materials

- Handout 25.2: Erase the Waste Choice Board
- Handout 28.1: Brainteaser C
- Student journals

Assessment

- Journal prompt

Procedures

1. Review the events from the previous lesson.
2. Show students Handout 28.1: Brainteaser C and ask them to solve it with a partner.
3. Explain that the answer is change over time.
4. **Anchor activity:** Tell students that their anchor activity today, if they finish working on their choice board activity before the end of class, is to talk with their PBL groups about how their thinking about trash has changed over time from the beginning of the unit to now.
5. Ask students if they have any questions about their choice board assignment.
6. Provide the rest of the class period for students to work.
7. Monitor and support students as they collaborate to finish their projects.
8. A few minutes before the class period ends, bring students back together as a whole group and explain the plan for the next class period:
   - students will share their completed choice board activities,
   - final points will be awarded, and
   - the winner of this episode of *Waste Warriors* will be declared.

9. **Journal prompt:** Ask students to respond to the following journal prompt: *Imagine that a reporter interviewing you about your experiences on the show asks you the following question: "What advice do you have for people watching at home who want to make change in their own communities, businesses, and households?"*

Name: ______________________ Date: ______________

HANDOUT 28.1

Brainteaser C

CHANGE

LESSON 28

LESSON 29

The Winner of Waste Warriors

Objectives

- Students will share their completed choice board projects with the class.
- Students will learn who the winner of the *Waste Warriors* competition is.

Materials

- Handout 2.3: Need to Know Board
- Handout 25.2: Erase the Waste Choice Board
- Handout 29.1: Key to the City Award
- Handout 29.2: $25,000 Prize Certificate
- Student journals

Assessments

- Handout 25.2: Erase the Waste Choice Board
- Journal prompt
- Need to Know Boards

Procedures

1. Review the events from the previous lesson.
2. Remind students that today they will share their choice board projects and find out who the winner of the competition is.
3. Review the expectations for the audience before presentations begin.
4. Ask for volunteers and begin the presentations.

TEACHER'S NOTE

While students are presenting, revisit the choice menu description and decide if the group earned one full extra point (if they chose a project worth one point), two full points (if they chose a project worth two points), or three full points (if they proposed a rigorous project of their own). Partial points can be awarded as well.

5. Thank students for their efforts and read the following message from the producers of the *Waste Warriors* show:

> The winner of the episode is always declared in the last 5 minutes of the show. It is typically a standard affair during which dramatic music is played to build the tension. Clips of the business owners and team members are shown to remind the audience of all that has transpired. Finally, after a short 10-second drum roll, the winner is announced. Today we will do something a little differently, however.

The mayor of the town has requested the opportunity to present each team with a Key to the City in honor of your amazing work. (Distribute Handout 29.1: Key to the City Award.) Thank you, Mayor, for your appreciation and the opportunity to visit your fair city. Now, on with the show. (Ask students to create a drum roll using their hands on their laps.) With no further ado, the winner of this episode of *Waste Warriors* is . . . (hold for dramatic effect and then announce the winner).

6. Congratulate the winner and provide the group with Handout 29.2: $25,000 Prize Certificate.

TEACHER'S NOTE

Many teachers regularly take photos of their students as they work and/or present projects. One great way to enhance the end of this *Waste Warriors* reality show episode is to prepare and play a real highlight reel of past projects and work sessions.

7. Explain to students that they will be taking their posttest tomorrow and, therefore, should review any notes, handouts, or journal entries they have collected over the course of the unit.
8. Ask students to get out their Need to Know Boards (Handout 2.3) they have been using since the beginning of the unit. Instruct students to get into their PBL groups one more time and record three important lessons they have learned.
9. Provide a chance for groups to share what they have learned.
10. **Journal prompt:** Ask students to complete the following journal prompt: *The winner of this episode of the competition will return to compete in the finale for the chance to win $100,000. Imagine this is the final challenge: Participants will travel abroad and provide feedback to three businesses in three countries over the course of 3 days. What would be your strategy for winning the $100,000?*

Name: ______________________________ Date: ______________

HANDOUT 29.1

Key to the City Award

To Whom It May Concern,

On this, the __________ day of ____________________, in the year 20 __________, I do solemnly bequeath to the undersigned an official Key to the City in recognition of your tireless efforts to "Erase the Waste and Turn Trash Into Cash."

You are always welcome in our town!

Sincerely,

Mayor ____

LESSON 29

Name: ______________________ Date: ______________

HANDOUT 29.1, continued

LESSON 29

Name: ______________________ Date: ______________

HANDOUT 29.2

$25,000 Prize Certificate

$25,000

THIS CERTIFICATE IS TO COMMEND

____

For Winning 1st Place in
***Waste Warriors* Episode 37**

Awarded the _____ Day of ____________, 20 _____.

____
Signed

LESSON 29

LESSON 30

Proving Proficiency

Objectives

- Students will continue to reflect on what they have learned throughout the unit.
- Students will take the final unit assessment.

Materials

- Student answers to Question 12 on Handout 1.1: Pretest
- Handout 30.1: Posttest
- Student journals

Assessments

- Handout 30.1: Posttest
- Journal prompt

Procedures

1. Review the events from the previous lesson.
2. Locate the pretests that students took at the beginning of the unit (Handout 1.1), and share with students the answers they wrote for Question 12 (i.e., What do you hope to learn during this unit?).
3. Ask students to talk with a partner about whether or not they did learn what they hoped.
4. Poll students and gather results.
5. Make a list of unanswered questions from the pretest and divide them up between small groups of students.
6. Provide 10 minutes for students to conduct research and find answers.
7. Take 5 minutes for groups of students to share out what they found.
8. Thank students for their efforts and distribute Handout 30.1: Posttest. Review the directions and provide the remainder of class time for students to work.
9. Collect and score the posttests.
10. Offer students the chance to compare their pretest answers and overall score with their posttest answers and overall score.
11. **Journal prompt:** Ask students to complete the following journal prompt: *Based on the growth I showed from pretest to posttest, the amount of change over time I exhibited is (insert a predicate adjective like large, substantial, minimal, etc.).*

Name: ______________________________ Date: ______________

HANDOUT 30.1

Posttest

Directions: Answer each question to the best of your ability.

1. Give an example of how your thinking about trash has changed over time.

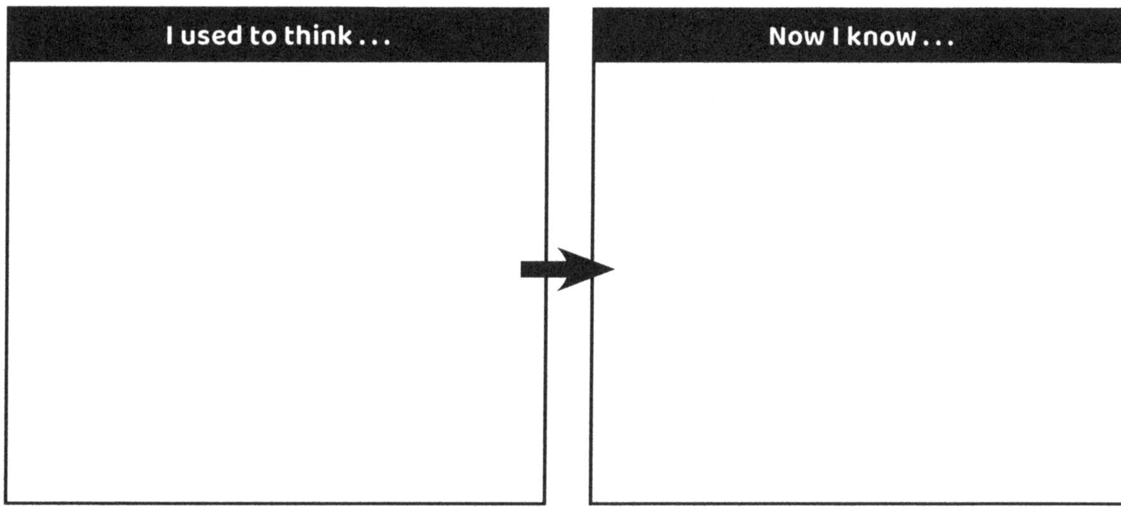

2. What is an environmental engineer?

3. List the four tools we can use to erase waste:

4. What does it mean to reimagine something?

Name: ______________________________ Date: ______________

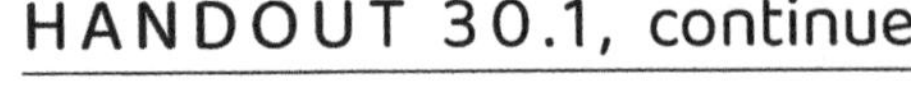

HANDOUT 30.1, continued

5. What is SCAMPER, and how would you apply it to an empty water bottle?

6. How many pounds of garbage does the average person in the United States create each day? (Please circle the best answer.)
   a. 1 pound
   b. 2–3 pounds
   c. 4–5 pounds
   d. 6–8 pounds

7. What are two ways you can reduce the amount of trash you produce each day?

8. Define the following terms in your own words:

   a. Throwaway society:

   b. Solid waste management:

   c. Overconsumption:

   d. Compostable:

   e. General ledger:

Name: ______________________________ Date: ______________

HANDOUT 30.1, continued

9. Complete the pie chart below so that it represents an estimate of how much of the garbage produced in the United States is of each type:

   - Metal
   - Plastic
   - Glass
   - Yard trimmings
   - Paper
   - Rubber, leather, fabric
   - Food scraps
   - Wood
   - Other

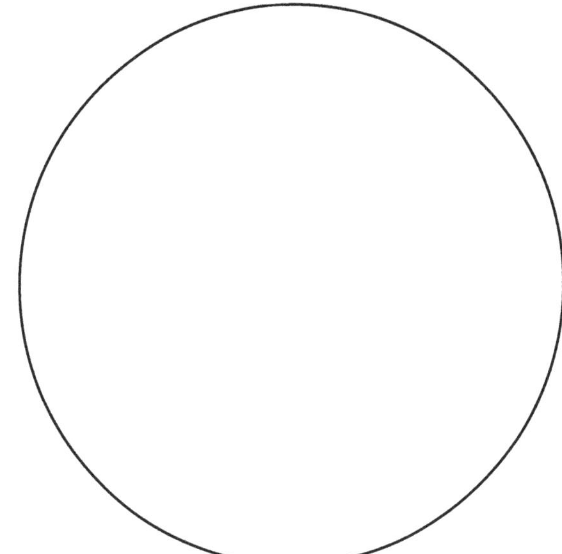

10. Give three reasons why plastic is such a problem around the world.

11. What are the steps involved in recycling a recyclable item of your choosing (e.g., tin can, plastic water bottle, etc.)?

12. What are two big ideas you will take away from this unit?

LESSON 30

References

Brown, L. (2019, April 11). *Plastic toys: Is it time we cut back?* BBC News. https://www.bbc.com/news/science-environment-47868871

Dell, J. (2020, April 8). *No 'away': Why is the U.S. still offshoring plastic waste around the world?* Basel Action Network. https://www.ban.org/news/2020/4/8/no-away-why-is-the-us-still-offshoring-plastic-waste-around-the-world#:~:text=Since%20exporting%20plastic%20waste%20is,other%20countries%20instead%20of%20China

Dine Green. (n.d.). *Waste reduction and recycling*. https://www.dinegreen.com/waste

Eberle, B. (1996). *Scamper: Games for imagination development*. Prufrock Press.

Goldberg, E. (2017, May 10). *There's a huge problem with kids' toys that no one's talking about.* HuffPost. https://www.huffpost.com/entry/your-kids-toys-are-killing-the-planet_n_58ffa383e4b0f5463a1a9472

Helms, K. J. (2016, June 6). *Power Knot: Study shows hotel guests average 2.2 pounds of waste per night*. https://www.prweb.com/releases/2016/06/prweb13464063.htm

Kaplan, S. (2009). The grid: A model to construct differentiated curriculum for the gifted. In J. S. Renzulli, E. J. Gubbins, K. S. McMillen, R. D. Eckert, & C. A. Little (Eds.), *Systems and models for developing programs for the gifted and talented* (2nd ed., pp. 235–251). Prufrock Press.

Kaplan, S. (2012, October). *Paving the way to the common core* [Keynote presentation]. Orange County Council for Gifted and Talented Education's 38th Annual Conference, University of California, Irvine, CA, United States.

National Association for Gifted Children. (2019). *2019 Pre-K–Grade 12 Gifted Programming Standards*. https://www.nagc.org/sites/default/files/standards/Intro%202019%20Programming%20Standards.pdf

Leahy, S. (2018, May). *How people make only a jar of trash a year*. National Geographic. https://www.nationalgeographic.com/science/article/zero-waste-families-plastic-culture

United Nations. (2018). *Our planet is drowning in plastic pollution—it's time for change!* https://www.unep.org/interactive/beat-plastic-pollution

U.S. Environmental Protection Agency. (n.d.-a). *National overview: Facts and figures on materials, waste and recycling*. https://www.epa.gov/facts-and-figures-about-materials-waste-and-recycling/national-overview-facts-and-figures-materials

U.S. Environmental Protection Agency. (n.d.-b). *Plastic: Specific-materials data*. https://www.epa.gov/facts-and-figures-about-materials-waste-and-recycling/plastics-material-specific-data#:~:text=In%202018%2C%20plastics%20generation%20was,measure%20the%20recycling%20of%20plastic

U.S. Environmental Protection Agency. (2016). *Municipal solid waste*. https://archive.epa.gov/epawaste/nonhaz/municipal/web/html

TheWorldCounts. (2021). *Tons of waste dumped on the planet*. https://www.theworldcounts.com/challenges/planet-earth/waste/global-waste-problem/stor

Appendix A

Recommended Reading

The Editors of TIME. (2020). TIME Sustainability: The practical, sustainable life [Special issue]. *TIME Magazine*.

Latham, D. (2011). *Garbage: Investigate what happens when you throw it out.* Nomad Press.

Su, S. (2018). *Zero waste: Simple life hacks to drastically reduce your trash.* Skyhorse Press.

Appendix B

Master Materials List

Lesson 1

- Butcher paper (approximately 10 feet long)
- Cleaned trash (10–20 items) (*Note.* Keep to use during Lesson 16.)
- Markers (several boxes for students to share)
- Tape (one roll)
- Small notebook for each student

Lesson 7

- Empty plastic bottle (1)

Lesson 9

- Highlighters (one per student) (*Note.* Keep to use during Lesson 13.)

Lesson 14

- 3" × 5" index cards (3–5 per student)

Lesson 15

- Dice (one or more)

Lesson 16

- Trash can
- Recycling container
- Cleaned trash from Lesson 1

Lesson 18

- Bubble wrap (12" per student)
- Paint brushes (one per student)
- Tempera paint (several colors)
- Scraps of paper (random collection)
- Sheets of clean paper (2–3 per student)

Lesson 20

- Various art supplies (e.g., glue, tape, scissors, glitter, construction paper)
- Various recyclable materials (e.g., cups, straws, bottles, boxes, cans)

Lesson 24

- Sticky notes (5 per small group of students)

About the Author

Jason S. McIntosh, Ph.D., is an experienced educator (24 years in the field) and passionate advocate for gifted education. He earned his doctorate in Gifted, Creative, and Talented Studies at Purdue's Gifted Education Research Institute in 2015 and is currently serving as a gifted coordinator and independent consultant. Since his time at Purdue, Jason has authored five NAGC Curriculum Studies Network Award-winning curriculum units (2016–2020) and hopes to write many more in the future. His latest project is the H.O.T. Spot, a weekly mini-magazine for curious kids, which provides in-depth exploration of a new high-interest topic each issue. To subscribe to the H.O.T. Spot, contact him for professional development services, or find out more about his latest curriculum projects, please visit his website at http://www.notmoreofthesame.com.

Common Core State Standards Alignment

Subject	Domain	Common Core State Standards
ELA	Reading Literature	RL.3.1 Ask and answer questions to demonstrate understanding of a text, referring explicitly to the text as the basis for the answers.
		RL.3.3 Describe characters in a story (e.g., their traits, motivations, or feelings) and explain how their actions contribute to the sequence of events.
		RL.4.10 By the end of the year, read and comprehend literature, including stories, dramas, and poetry, in the grades 4–5 text complexity band proficiently, with scaffolding as needed at the high end of the range.

Subject	Domain	Common Core State Standards
ELA, *continued*	Reading Informational Text	RI.3.2 Determine the main idea of a text; recount the key details and explain how they support the main idea.
		RI.4.3 Explain events, procedures, ideas, or concepts in a historical, scientific, or technical text, including what happened and why, based on specific information in the text.
		RI.4.7 Interpret information presented visually, orally, or quantitatively (e.g., in charts, graphs, diagrams, time lines, animations, or interactive elements on Web pages) and explain how the information contributes to an understanding of the text in which it appears.
		RI.4.9 Integrate information from two texts on the same topic in order to write or speak about the subject knowledgeably.
	Reading Foundational Skills	RF.4.4 Read with sufficient accuracy and fluency to support comprehension.
	Writing	W.3.8 Recall information from experiences or gather information from print and digital sources; take brief notes on sources and sort evidence into provided categories.
		W.3.10 Write routinely over extended time frames (time for research, reflection, and revision) and shorter time frames (a single sitting or a day or two) for a range of discipline-specific tasks, purposes, and audiences.
		W.4.1 Write opinion pieces on topics or texts, supporting a point of view with reasons and information.
		W.4.2 Write informative/explanatory texts to examine a topic and convey ideas and information clearly.

Subject	Domain	Common Core State Standards
ELA, *continued*	Writing, *continued*	W.4.7 Conduct short research projects that build knowledge through investigation of different aspects of a topic.
		W.4.8 Recall relevant information from experiences or gather relevant information from print and digital sources; take notes and categorize information, and provide a list of sources.
		W.4.9 Draw evidence from literary or informational texts to support analysis, reflection, and research.
	Speaking and Listening	SL.3.3 Ask and answer questions about information from a speaker, offering appropriate elaboration and detail.
		SL.4.1 Engage effectively in a range of collaborative discussions (one-on-one, in groups, and teacher-led) with diverse partners on grade 4 topics and texts, building on others' ideas and expressing their own clearly.
		SL.4.3 Identify the reasons and evidence a speaker provides to support particular points.
		SL.4.4 Report on a topic or text, tell a story, or recount an experience in an organized manner, using appropriate facts and relevant, descriptive details to support main ideas or themes; speak clearly at an understandable pace.
	Language	L.4.1 Demonstrate command of the conventions of standard English grammar and usage when writing or speaking.
		L.4.2 Demonstrate command of the conventions of standard English capitalization, punctuation, and spelling when writing.
		L.4.5 Demonstrate understanding of figurative language, word relationships, and nuances in word meanings.

Subject	Domain	Common Core State Standards
ELA, *continued*	Language, *continued*	L.4.6 Acquire and use accurately grade-appropriate general academic and domain-specific words and phrases, including those that signal precise actions, emotions, or states of being (e.g., quizzed, whined, stammered) and that are basic to a particular topic (e.g., wildlife, conservation, and endangered when discussing animal preservation).
Math	Operations and Algebraic Thinking	3.OA.B Understand properties of multiplication and the relationship between multiplication and division.
		3.OA.D Solve problems involving the four operations, and identify and explain patterns in arithmetic.
	Number and Operations—Base Ten	4.NBT.B Use place value understanding and properties of operations to perform multi-digit arithmetic.
		5.NBT.A Understand the place value system.
	Measurement and Data	3.MD.A Solve problems involving measurement and estimation.
		4.MD.A Solve problems involving measurement and conversion of measurements.
	Ratios and Proportional Relationships	6.RP.A Understand ratio concepts and use ratio reasoning to solve problems.
	The Number System	6.NS.B Compute fluently with multi-digit numbers and find common factors and multiples.
	Statistics and Probability	6.SP.B Summarize and describe distributions.

Next Generation Science Standards Alignment

Grade Level	Next Generation Science Standards
3	3-LS4-4. Make a claim about the merit of a solution to a problem caused when the environment changes and the types of plants and animals that live there may change.
4	4-PS3-4. Apply scientific ideas to design, test, and refine a device that converts energy from one form to another.
	4-ESS3-1. Obtain and combine information to describe that energy and fuels are derived from natural resources and their uses affect the environment.
	4-ESS3-2. Generate and compare multiple solutions to reduce the impacts of natural Earth processes on humans.
5	5-LS2-1. Develop a model to describe the movement of matter among plants, animals, decomposers, and the environment.

Grade Level	Next Generation Science Standards
5, *continued*	5-ESS3-1. Obtain and combine information about ways individual communities use science ideas to protect the Earth's resources and environment.
3–5	3-5-ETS1-1. Define a simple design problem reflecting a need or a want that includes specified criteria for success and constraints on materials, time, or cost.
	3-5-ETS1-3. Plan and carry out fair tests in which variables are controlled and failure points are considered to identify aspects of a model or prototype that can be improved.